TITANS OF THE AMERICAN STAGE

"We love men flaming toward the stars."

—Eugene O'Neill
from *Lazarus Laughed*

TITANS OF THE AMERICAN STAGE

Edwin Forrest
the Booths, the O'Neills

by DALE SHAW

THE WESTMINSTER PRESS
Philadelphia

ISBN 0–664–32501–7

LIBRARY OF CONGRESS CATALOG CARD NO. 73–158123

PHOTO CREDITS: Museum of the City of New York, pp. 101, 111; Print Collection, Free Library of Philadelphia, p. 19; Theatre Collection, Free Library of Philadelphia, pp. 13, 16, 21, 29, 32, 33, 35, 41, 50, 53, 65, 77, 78, 83, 88, 106, 117, 118, 137, 145, 153.

PUBLISHED BY THE WESTMINSTER PRESS ®

PHILADELPHIA, PENNSYLVANIA

PRINTED IN THE UNITED STATES OF AMERICA

The prompter's hand is on his bell;
The coming heroes, lovers, kings,
Are idly lounging in the wings;
Behind the curtain's mystic fold
The glowing future lies unrolled.

—Bret Harte
Address at opening of the
California Theatre
San Francisco
January 19, 1870

Contents

Introduction

THREE NAMES dominate American theater: Forrest, Booth, and O'Neill. One might easily find their counterparts in the theater of England, Russia, or France: men obsessed, men who changed things, men memorable for eccentricity, departure, persistence, and headline-making. Men who drank heavily of the cup of life and sometimes the cup of wine. Men profoundly sensitive, men of deep passion.

Let it not be misunderstood that in grouping Edwin Forrest, Junius Brutus Booth and his remarkable sons John Wilkes and Edwin, and James O'Neill and his son Eugene, the object is to spotlight men of the theater whose perversity struck high above the national average. It would be better to observe that despite unfortunate tendencies, they made their mark on theater history through prodigious work, and in the exercise of true talent. Few people can respond to adversity with greatness, to suffering with inspiration. Two Booths succeeded despite their infirmities; John Wilkes succumbed to his. Forrest, had he been one jot more headstrong, never could have encouraged the cooperation of managers and actors as he did. Alcohol barely failed to unhinge James O'Neill and his son Eugene, but liquor did destroy his actor son, James, Jr.

The successes and struggles chronicled here, then, are a tribute to what has been accomplished by several of the more Herculean and at times less civilized men of our short theatrical era, in the face of temptations and weaknesses that daily bring ordinary people to complete destruction.

Past the temptation to gossip, we can find in the lives of these titans of the American stage enduring inspiration.

Their lives are joined to span a century of progress in the theater of a young nation. Their lives and those of the thousands of show people who supported them are the history of that theater.

D.S.

1
Edwin Forrest

YOUNG EARLY AMERICANS who dreamed of the glamour and excitement of going on the stage—and many did—dreamed in private. When the time was ripe, they packed a bag in the night and ran away.

One Reverend Gardiner Spring, upon finding that his daughter had merely *attended* a theatrical performance on a Saturday, denounced her from the pulpit on Sunday: "Eliza Spring, having recently visited one of those profane and sinful places of carnal recreation, commonly called theatres, is hereby cut off from the communion of the Church of Christ."

Ministers in general continued to preach against sinful impersonations and the creation of false idols. In 1774, the Continental Congress discouraged "every species of extravagance and dissipation, especially all horse-racing, and all kinds of gaming, cock-fighting, exhibitions of shews, plays and other expensive diversions and entertainments."

As early as the 1730's, actors had worked in New York, Richmond, and Charleston, delighting the brave, the foolish, and the entertainment-starved with their hearty if flimsy productions. These strolling players, who carried their scenery on their backs when their horses mired, were Englishmen who had caught the wanderlust, grown heady with the idea of a new land where competition was nil. A few had fled from debt back home or from personal trouble of a discouraging and unmentionable nature.

Lewis Hallam's company, starting here in 1752, thrived by keeping on the move. It opened with *The Merchant of Venice* in Williamsburg, Virginia. George Washington was in the audience. He was twenty. Washington was not surprised to find all the actors English; all good actors seemed to be visiting Englishmen. Most of them vanished like the leaves when autumn came.

But the Hallams stayed. So did Thomas Abthorpe Cooper and George Frederick Cooke, whose reputations survived the Revolution, and who helped form the barricade against which an imaginative young American, Edwin Forrest, might test his talents.

Edwin Forrest was the first star in America's theatrical firmament, her first major actor, a man who broke the English monopoly of our stage. By 1828, though only twenty-two, he had won the acclaim of audiences and critics.

In a career lasting more than forty years, Forrest left his mark on acting style, helped many players in their profession, and commissioned dramas on American themes by American writers. But he was an unusual and dynamic character, headstrong, egocentric.

His beginnings were humble. His father, proud but poor, served as a runner at Stephen Girard's bank in Philadelphia. His mother, Rebecca, was the daughter of German immigrants who settled near Philadelphia about 1750. She had met William Forrest, then thirty-seven, when he was struggling with a small business in Trenton, New Jersey. He told her he had come from Cooniston, Edinburgh County, Scotland, and that he was a hard worker but the luck was not running right. She said that she might help him succeed.

But she had not.

William Forrest in fact had lost his strength; he suffered from chronic tuberculosis. Five children were born to the marriage—three sons and two daughters. Edwin, the fourth child, was thin, narrow-chested, with dark, appealing eyes and thick, dark, curly hair. Because of his weakness, his parents feared he would die young of the "consumption," as tuberculosis was then called.

One might see him standing on the narrow stone walk on Cedar Street, a street full of horses and sparrows in the Southwark slum of Philadelphia, in 1813. He was about seven, waiting in the lazy heat of an early summer evening for his father to come from work.

His mother might call from the window, "Ed-win, mind you stay put, and don't play with those others."

These cautionings must have been ritual. Once he had heard her say, "My Ned, he's a weak child." He had overheard his father worrying, "We fear she shall never be able to raise Edwin." The thin ones got consumption, and he was thin. Not very comforting to a small boy.

He would stay put, with a shrug, skipping cracks one-footed or reciting

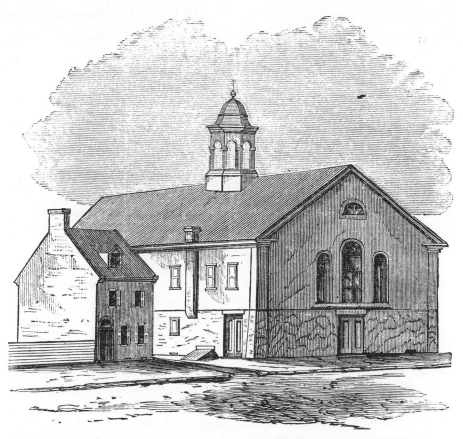

Charles Porter, of the Old Southwark Theatre, Philadelphia, gave eleven-year-old Forrest his first part, as a girl, in *Rudolph; or, the Robber of Calabria*. From a sketch by Charles Durang, drawn for *The Sunday Dispatch*

rhymes to pass the time. Boys or more likely girls might gather to listen, because he knew so many words and such long verses. Some bad ones too. He had a special ability, his mother said, for remembering lines.

In the cooling day the vendors would come, screeching down alleyways, the swelling, sweating sides of their plodding horses almost brushing Edwin, the great rusty rims of their wagons clanking close to his toes.

A peddler selling ice and syrup must be resisted. Edwin had no money. Finally his father would come, laboring, often coughing, hunched over, taking short, painful steps, but brightening when he saw Edwin, offering a happy handclasp, and something from his pocket, a candy or a cracker. He told his son of the great goings-on at the bank, of the grand Stephen

Girard who went to sea a cabin boy and now was a millionaire, of the investors and railroad men and steel men who came and went as thick as flies. It was all very impressive to a simple bank messenger, and to his son electrifying.

The Forrests believed in education and books. Their great pleasure was in listening to the children recite. Edwin outshone them all. He was as quick with his tongue indoors as he was outdoors on the street.

"I am going to have you meet someone who likes good reading," said his father. "Someone from the bank." That someone turned out to be Alexander Wilson, a noted ornithologist, and probably a depositor. Wilson was impressed, recommending Lemuel G. White, a downtown elocutionist. Why, the boy showed such powers of speech that he might someday fill the pulpit of the best church in the city!

William Forrest settled on theology for Edwin, seeing in it nothing but security. Edwin got his speech lessons week by week through scrimping and saving. His voice grew stronger and to some more unbearable. If his brothers and sisters complained, they were reminded that a minister of the gospel was in the making.

It took one of those peculiar turns of fate to part Edwin from his father's ambition. One day he attended a demonstration of nitrous oxide, or laughing gas, at Tivoli Garden Theatre. He was given a whiff and recited for ten minutes. When he snapped out of it, Col. John Swift, later mayor of Philadelphia, put his arm around the boy and said, "This lad has the germ of tragic greatness."

Swift is credited with having become Edwin's sponsor, influencing him toward the stage. Charles Porter, manager of the famous Southwark Theatre, became a major influence. Not long before the other incident, when Edwin was eleven, Porter needed someone young in a hurry to play Rosalia in *Rudolph; or, the Robber of Calabria*. (At that time boys often played girls' parts.) Finding Edwin hanging around the theater, he asked, "Are you the schoolboy spouter?"

"Yes," said Edwin. Porter then explained the emergency and told the boy that since he would be reclining on a couch throughout the play and could hide the promptbook, he need not learn any lines.

Edwin's father took the news skeptically. This was a far cry from theology; all the same, he thought, it could be a useful and terrifying experience.

The Robber of Calabria was a rousing drama. Edwin was eager and nervous. He had never before been backstage in any theater. At the South-wark he poked his nose into narrow dressing rooms, saw the wigs and greasepaint, the dirty costumes that looked so splendid under brighter lights, and listened to the rough talk of actors and stage workmen rushing to get things ready for the show.

They plopped a wig on his head. A bright length of window curtain was tied around him as a dress. But before they could array him on Rosalia's divan, Edwin had a chance to peek out through the stage curtains. What he saw amazed and thrilled him.

There were ladies and gentlemen by the hundreds waiting to watch him. There was the general populace, gay and noisy, in their lower-priced sec-tion—people like his father and mother, perhaps, who had saved for the occasion.

In special boxes, elevated above the pit, were seated a few persons of special importance, none of whom he recognized. They seemed impatient and slightly bored.

One box was emblazoned with the seal of the United States—the fa-miliar eagle clutching arrows and an olive branch. In that box, Edwin knew, President Washington himself had sat many times.

The Southwark Theatre, built in 1766, had been used by the British General Howe, whose soldiers put on plays. In those days, Major John André, who later was hanged as a British spy, painted scenery and played small parts. There was a piece of scenery still around which André had painted—a flat of shrubbery, chipped and dusty, used in *The Old Soldier* in 1802, and still pressed into service occasionally.

The play began well. Edwin, reclining on a divan, read his lines prop-erly and in as high a voice as possible. But gradually the footlights grew dimmer, and he could not make out the words. In panic, he sat up, leaning toward the candles on the side, which were brighter. As he did so, his booted feet thudded to the floor.

A shout rang out from one of Edwin's friends, "The gentle Rosalia wears clodhoppers! And heavy wool stockings!"

The audience roared, laughed, hissed, and applauded. Edwin threw down his book, hitched up his skirt, and fled the theater.

He was furious. He had made a fool of himself, and he must undo the damage. Running straight home, he put on a harlequin costume that his sisters had made for him to wear during recitations, rushed back to the theater, bolted onstage during an intermission and read David Garrick's

Walnut Street Theatre.

Monday Evening, November 27, 1820.

Will be presented a Tragedy, (in 5 acts,) called

DOUGLAS;

Or, the Noble Shepherd.

WRITTEN BY MR. HOME. *Edwin Forrest;*

Young Norval, . . by a Young Gentleman of this City
Lord Randolph, Mr. WHEATLY. Glenalvon Mr. WOOD. Old Norval, Mr. WARREN.
Norval's Servant, Mr. MARTIN. First Officer, Mr. SCRIVENER. Second Officer, Mr. CARTER.
Third Officer, Mr. PARKER.
Lady Randolph, Mrs. WILLIAMS. Anna, Mrs. JEFFERSON.

After the Tragedy, the favourite Ballet of

Little Red Riding Hood.

Lubin, Miss C. DURANG. Wolfe, (the Robber) Mr. C. DURANG. Old Man, Mr. MURRAY.
Villagers, Messrs. SCRIVENER, MARTIN, PARKER, &c. Grand Mother, Mr. CARTER.
Red Riding Hood, Miss K. DURANG. Anna, Miss SEYMOUR. Janet, Mrs. CARTER.
Ellen, Mrs. RICHARDSON. Phœbe, Miss HATHWELL. Colinette, Mrs. BLOXTON.

In the course of the Ballet the favourite Dances to the Airs of

Paddy O'Rafferty, Coolin, &c. &c.

To conclude with

A GENERAL DANCE.

To which will be added the favourite Farce of the

Budget of Blunders.

Mr. Growley, Mr. HERBERT. Doctor Dablancour, Mr. BLISSETT.
Doctor Smugface, Mr. JEFFERSON. Captain Belgrave, Mr. BAKER. Tom, Mr. CARTER.
Servant to Dablancour, Mr. PARKER. Post Boy, Mr. MARTIN.
Sophy, Miss SEYMOUR. Bridget, Mrs. FRANCIS. Deborah, Mrs. BLOXTON.

In consequence of the indisposition of Mrs. WOOD, the Farce of Three
Weeks after Marriage is unavoidably postponed.

Ladies and Gentlemen are respectfully reminded that there are two flights of Stairs to the Boxes: by using
one for entering the Theatre and the other for leaving it, much accommodation may be gained.

The Melo-Drama of the HEART OF MID-LOTHIAN; or, the Lily of St. Leonards, will be immediately
revived---Also, the RUFFIAN BOY.

In preparation the new pieces of VIRGINIUS---EXCHANGE NO ROBBERY---and a new interesting
Drama called the FATE of CALAS, &c. &c.

Gentlemen holding season Tickets are respectfully requested to write their names at the Box door, or leave
a card.

N. B. CHECKS NOT TRANSFERABLE.

Places in the Boxes may be taken of Mr. Johnson, at the Box Office, from 10 till 2, and on days of performance from 10 till 4 o'clock.

BOX, ONE DOLLAR---PIT, SEVENTY-FIVE CENTS---GALLERY, FIFTY CENTS.
The doors will be opened at half past 5 o'clock, and the curtain will rise at half past 6, precisely.
A few Season Tickets for sale by Thomas De Silver, No. 255, Market street.

Billed simply as "A Young Gentleman of this City," Edwin played Young
Norval in John Home's melodrama *Douglas*. Original playbill

"The Harlequinade," without invitation, but to much applause. He walked offstage balancing on his hands! A very angry Porter turned up right behind him.

"He chased me out and down the street," Forrest said in later years. "But from that moment my destiny was sealed. I felt that I was to be an actor, and an actor I would be, come what may."

Edwin had grown stronger with his acrobatics; he added wrestling and weight lifting. His chest filled, his shoulders straightened. However, his father had grown weaker.

From his sickbed, William Forrest could hear his son reading aloud the winged words of Shakespeare, challenging and vibrant. *What a preacher!* he thought.

Edwin would stop, sometimes, to listen to his father's racking cough. When the coughing did not subside, he would go to his father's side.

Fatherless at thirteen, Edwin Forrest emerged from the black days of mourning obsessed with physical culture, acting, and survival. In his mind his father's death was linked with poverty, so Edwin felt that he must become rich as well as strong.

He received his first test on November 27, 1820, an off night, since it was Monday, at the Walnut Street Theatre, Philadelphia. Billed simply as "a Young Gentleman of this City," Forrest, then fourteen, played the role of Young Norval in John Home's *Douglas,* a standard piece of the time. In this thriller, Norval, betrayed by the villain and stabbed by his stepfather, dies in the arms of his long-lost mother.

After the performance, Forrest stalked the streets, waiting for newspaper notices. He ripped the papers apart until he found what he wanted —William Duane's review.

"Of the part of Norval," said the critic carefully, "we must say that we were much surprised at the excellence of his elocution, his self-possession in speech and gesture, and a voice that, without straining, was of such volume and fine tenor as to carry every tone and articulation to the remotest corner of the theatre."

Forrest danced on air.

He would overlook Duane's reference to "some . . . stiffness in moments of passive action," a prophetic comment on a lasting tendency to fire and brimstone. The theater managers encouraged Forrest with new parts in *Lovers' Vows* and *The Mountaineers,* and *Douglas.* For the four performances, he received the handsome sum of $39.

The theater manager, William Wood, noted that Forrest was a "well-grown young man, with a noble figure, unusually developed for his age." The principal actors considered his performance "far beyond any they had ever witnessed from a novice."

Edwin discovered, however, that such praise could be accompanied by a dismissal.

"Why are you firing me?" he asked, hurt and confused.

"My boy," said William Wood sadly, "I do not yet detect sufficient public enthusiasm. When all's said, the public decides."

Forrest did not have to have it explained to him that he was not a "star." For one thing, to be a *star,* you must be *English*—and he, as his father had sworn, was an American, product of two peoples, the Scotch and the German. He keenly shared his father's patriotism. Now, as an American, he must become a star himself.

In practice, the star was the actor who received feature billing. In hand-bills or advertisements, his name appeared first, often accompanied by decorative stars to set it off. A star might be affixed to his dressing-room door if, in those rough days, the theater had any dressing rooms.

Edwin Forrest started toward his goal. Renting the tiny, dilapidated Prune Street Theatre, he staged his own production of *Richard III,* playing Richard, of course. The amateur show drew a good house, said a critic, and small pecuniary gain.

Thomas Abthorpe Cooper was a star. Like the others who toured America, he was English, and had become old and rich, with no native player to rival him. Forrest traveled miles, often on foot, to see Cooper perform.

Cooper moved from engagement to engagement by private carriage. He dined in style. One night he looked up from a plate of chicken to see young Forrest standing there before him.

Edwin swiftly recited his credits. Cooper was impressed. Forrest was extremely good-looking, spoke pleasantly. Hard work, plenty of study—those were the credentials, Cooper told him. Forrest thought he was being advised to play bit parts, to start over. He turned on his heel.

Theater managers throughout the East read letters from an unknown self-proclaiming actor named Edwin Forrest who promised all sorts of attendance miracles. These letters went unanswered.

The star system was deep-rooted. Even two decades after Edwin's frustrated attempts to find parts, Walt Whitman, Edgar Allan Poe, and many other American authors criticized the star system and related abuses. Whitman contended that reviewers were "the slaves of the paid puff system," and that "English managers, English actors, and English plays . . . must be allowed to die away among us, as usurpers of our stage. The drama of this country can be the mouthpiece of freedom, refinement, liberal philanthropy, beautiful love for all our brethren. . . . With all our servility to foreign fashions, there is at the heart of the American masses . . . a lurking propensity toward what is original, and has a stamped American character of its own."

Young Forrest, much as he resented the English who stole the fanfare, was faced with stark poverty. He worked sixty hours a week as a clerk to help his sisters and mother, who had opened an unsuccessful millinery shop. His brother Lorman had gone to sea, never to be heard from. His brother William was to die young.

The Walnut Street Theatre, Philadelphia, as it looked in 1820 when Edwin Forrest played his first real dramatic role at fourteen. The theater looks much the same today. Drawn by C. Burton, New York. Engraved and printed by Fenner Sears & Co., 1831

Late in the summer of his sixteenth year Forrest was forced to inspect his resources. A life of clerking seemed to lie ahead.

Then one day the post brought an answer to one of his many letters. Joshua Collins and William Jones, owners of theaters in Pittsburgh, Lexington (Kentucky), and Cincinnati, might add him to their touring company. First they must hear him.

Forrest auditioned before Jones.

"You are a fine specimen of manly youth," Jones said.

Edwin's chest swelled with pride.

"Your bearing is strong, your eyes are steady," said the promoter. "Your voice is clear and deep."

Edwin held his breath.

"We shall warrant you $8 per week—"

Edwin gulped.

"And let it be understood that you shall play, without question, whatever parts in which you are cast, no matter how high—or how *low*. Is that understood?"

"Yes, sir," said Forrest gratefully, remembering the advice old Cooper had given: "You must not try to mount the ladder of fame by skips," he had said. "You must be willing to go up slowly, rung by rung."

In fact, Forrest found the first rung in Pittsburgh. After hundreds of miles of a bone-bruising stagecoach ride over rocky roads, he found himself playing Young Norval in *Douglas,* as he had at the Walnut Street Theatre in Philadelphia.

With a difference.

Dying in the arms of his long-lost mother, Forrest now glanced out on a sea of black umbrellas. The theater roof leaked like a sieve, and playgoers had come prepared.

Forrest faithfully wrote letters home.

Dear Mother:

Pittsburgh is three hundred miles from Philadelphia. It is a sort of London in miniature, very black and smoky. . . . The theatre is very old. . . . Give my respects to all my friends, and write as early as possible, and pray pay the postage, as I am out of funds. I expect the managers by the next stage.

Your affectionate son,
Edwin Forrest

In another letter, he wrote, "I miss you, dear, dear mother, more than

Thomas Abthorpe Cooper, British star, whom Forrest admired, urged plenty of study and hard work on the boy

words can give out." After all, he was not yet seventeen, and his new life was no bed of daisies.

The troupe struggled for recognition in a stolid, industrial town of practical souls. One night's receipts totaled $7. However, Collins and Jones were blooming with optimism. Westward lay throngs starved for entertainment.

Down the Ohio by flatboat, they floated dreamily along the frontier's major highway. Warm sun, crisp nights, the hooting of owls on river-banks. This was a better life.

Then joltingly they traveled seventy-five miles overland on rock-studded rutty roads to Lexington, Kentucky, where Forrest climbed limply down before a theater that resembled a brewery, which it had been. Well, the roof would be watertight.

By mid-December the company had fully prepared *Hamlet, The Merchant of Venice,* and *King Lear.* Forrest held minor parts, but he hand-tooled them. His fellow actors were particularly flabbergasted by his insistence that he read each line as it had been written by the author. Everyone else thought you were blessed if you came fairly close, and that your variations were probably improvements.

Even in his youth, Forrest had recognized the power of the play as literature. Yet, as an actor, he played to and encouraged audiences who loved the spectacle of personality, ranted lines, and dramatic stage sets. If the play included the simulation of a thunder-and-lightning storm, that fact would appear on the handbills in letters almost as large as the feature player's name.

The Lexington weather did not help Forrest's prospects—it was noted as the coldest in Kentucky within living memory. Theater patrons were requested "not to smoke segars in the Theatre." Attendance sagged.

On February 26, the Cincinnati *Advertiser* announced that the troupe was headed that way. The writer "perceived with pleasure" that "many rich theatrical repasts" were in store for his city. Early notices mentioned a "comer" named Forrest. Collins and Jones had raised him to $12 a week, in reward for his performance in *Marion—or the Hero of Lake George.* Edwin seemed unusually strong in this patriotic drama built around a Revolutionary incident.

However, if Cincinnati newspapers were eager, its rough citizens were not. Forrest was required to dance, sing comic songs, and turn somersaults and handsprings to pack the house.

From time to time, he was permitted to act "tragic personages." One night he distinguished himself as the daughter of a broken-down soldier. While the father played the fiddle, Forrest wailed in falsetto:

> Oh, cru-el was my parients as tored my love from me;
> And cru-el was the great big ship as took him off to sea;
> And cru-el was the capitaine, was the bo'sain, and the men,
> As didn't care a shillin' if we never met again.

The company's funds held out for six weeks, Forrest's prospects appearing dimmer by the day. However, good fortune smiled in the form of William Henry Harrison, former Ohio congressman and future senator and President. He admired the young actor and offered him helpful advice, insisting he board at the home of a friend, Widow Bryson, rather than endure the precarious lodging of his fellow actors—where harm might befall him.

Forrest accepted. He was a good listener too—eating up Harrison's stories of service under "Mad Anthony" Wayne at Fallen Timbers in 1794 when the Shawnees were routed, and his victory over Tecumseh at Tippecanoe in 1811. Harrison had been the first governor of the Territory of Indiana and Superintendent of Indian Affairs. Talking far into the night, he filled Forrest with an interest in the Red Man that lasted a lifetime. Harrison also gave the actor many helpful personal connections, for he admired Forrest's acrobatic skill, strength, and theatrical promise. So when Collins and Jones announced that the traveling company was dissolved, bankrupt, Forrest faced the future with uncommon good humor.

Adrift, as free as the wind, living in wagons, barns, or on the kindness of townspeople, Forrest and his associates plied their profession in the cities and villages of the then "Far West." When necessary, he played the clown or acrobat; for a time he joined a circus.

Two years on the road brought him back at last to Lexington, Kentucky, where theater patrons were still prohibited from smoking "segars." However, the weather was warmer, and so was his reception. Carrying Harrison's recommendation like a badge, he was able to ingratiate himself with Thomas Clay, son of Henry Clay, the famous senator and orator. Soon they were fast friends.

Forrest confided to Clay that Horace Holley, president of the local Transylvania College, a man of unusually inquiring mind, insisted that medical science be separated from church doctrine, and that human behavior be put on a scientific basis.

Tom Clay scratched his head.

Edwin explained that under Holley's persuasion he had decided to apply scientific principle to the art of acting. He must model a character on *character*. In the same breath, he mentioned King Lear, whose insanity had baffled many a portrayer. Clay understood: Forrest had in mind Clay's brother, Theodore, who in fits of derangement supposed himself to be George Washington. At other times his "spells" were more unpleasant, if not violent. Forrest was permitted to study Theodore Clay, and as a result his understanding of Lear increased.

Soon an offer came to play in New Orleans, at regular wages, thirteen hundred and fifty miles downriver by flatboat. Why not? Forrest was eighteen, a full five feet ten inches, sinewy as an ox. Audiences were already reacting to his physical appearance, his long, wavy black hair and dark, unhesitating eyes. He saw in the romantic southern city an unequaled opportunity.

New Orleans had enjoyed theater since 1791. James H. Caldwell, the principal impresario, an Englishman, had played first in Charleston, but ignoring the dangers of malaria and yellow fever, he was drawn to the Mississippi River port by its turbulent wealth.

Caldwell had heard of Forrest, and hired him for his new American Theatre on Camp Street, not far from Canal Street. Forrest could scarcely believe his eyes when he first saw this showplace. Built of solid brick, it thrust four marble piers toward the street, and these in turn lifted castiron fire pots skyward. On the night of his arrival, Edwin forgot his weariness at the sight of yellow flames flying in the wind, while flickering reflections shone on the polished surfaces of a broad marble stairway.

The pit and three galleries seated one thousand. There were forty-two boxes containing mahogany chairs covered in red velvet.

The young man who had slept in barns and fields adjusted rapidly to these surprises. He was flattered when the condescending Caldwell introduced him to New Orleans high society, but their fine manners and probing questions put him off-balance. He did not know that many a host had a background similar to his. At any rate, Forrest claimed a distaste for society. It was all frosting—the fancy dance, the formal introduction, the sudden and serious lapse into French when anyone might be discussing *his* rusticity.

It was a short walk to the waterfront, to the houses of pleasure, to the gambling rooms—a muddy walk too. Caldwell had built the American Theatre on marshy ground not far from the river, and in wet weather it had to be reached across planks placed athwart flatboats. In the free-swinging ways of a lower level of society, Forrest found release from the tensions of his craft and his ambition.

Caldwell gave him small parts. Even Richard in *Richard III* was re-written so as to diminish his importance. Jane Placide played the Queen. Lovely Jane. Edwin added to his worries by falling in love with her.

Forrest's cronies were James Bowie of knife-fighting fame, Captain Graham, a gambling, drinking river man, and a variety of Indian fighters, desperadoes, and duelists, as well as an Indian chief known as Push-ma-ta-ha, a friend of Bowie's. Forrest told them all of his love for Jane.

For two years, Forrest tasted this good life, grumbled as Caldwell slowly but surely let him find his speed, then cut him back again. All too seldom, he played opposite Jane. But if he loved her in silence, in deference to the feelings of his employer, he turned on his companions the full steam of his emotion.

"Thy spell, O Love, is elysium to my soul," he would read to the gentle-men gathered at the bar. "Freely I yield me to thy sweet control." What did the boys think of that?

"Put it in the paper!" they chorused.

So he did, cleverly persuading the editor of the *Louisiana Advertiser* to allow him space. However, he lacked courage to explain this and other verses to Jane.

She had come from Charleston as a singer and dancer, and she was older than he. Now as "Queen of the Drama in New Orleans," her looks had benumbed the critics, save one, who stated that "her only fault is that her shrieks of horror are too loud."

Forrest kept his love to himself so far as Caldwell was concerned until Caldwell insisted that he and not Edwin would play opposite Jane in *Twelfth Night*. Words were exchanged, words left unrecorded. Next day, the *Advertiser* carried the following personal announcement:

> Whereas James H. Caldwell has wronged and insulted me and refused me the satisfaction of a gentleman, I hereby denounce him as a scoun-drel and post him as a coward.—Edwin Forrest.

Forrest waited a day or two for reaction, alarmed at what he had done, yet sure that the older man had sense enough to avoid a deadly rival. Soon, though, sensible Edwin departed for the wild north country to relax with Push-ma-ta-ha, bent on studying the ways of the young chief. He would always possess this capacity for avoiding frustrating problems by immersing himself in the study of emotion and character, and Indian ways held considerable appeal. For two months in encampment, Forrest absorbed the Choctaw's life.

Deciding to return to Philadelphia, Edwin boarded a coastal sloop. Three days out of port, he took advantage of windless weather by disrobing and plunging into the mirrorlike sea. Several times Forrest circled the pretty sailing ship while passengers applauded. Suddenly, cries of alarm replaced the shouts of approval. Men pointed behind him. Turning his head, he saw, a considerable distance away, the black dorsal fin of a cruising shark.

Later, Forrest held after-dinner guests spellbound, telling how he clambered up the anchor chain a few feet ahead of the toothy fish, how he lay on the deck exhausted and relieved, making careful mental notes on that extreme emotion, terror. His powers of observation were already those of the mature actor.

2

The Challenger

EDWIN FORREST sailed into the port of Philadelphia in 1825, a man.

He found his mother well, her eyes brimming with tears of gratitude and admiration, and the city's theatrical trade in the blackest doldrums. However, he had written to William Conway, an actor who had guided him in New Orleans, and who had obtained a place for him at the new Pearl Street Theatre, Albany, New York. It was a fine house, financed by Stephen Van Rensselaer, last of the Dutch patroons. There Edwin would play Iago to Edmund Kean's Othello. It was Kean, the English star, who could catapult Forrest to stardom.

With surprising smoothness, Edwin fell into tempo with the more experienced player. Like Forrest, Kean had been a sickly child who compensated through acrobatics and muscular training. However, he was not used to the rude style of most of his American associates in the company.

Edwin had been given the role of Iago, the devilish subverter of Othello, and to the portrayal he added a disturbing new quality. After the performance, Kean leaped into Forrest's dressing room and shouted, "In the name of God, boy, where did you get *that?*"

Forrest replied, "It is something of my own."

"Well!" said Kean jubilantly. "Everybody who speaks the part hereafter must do it just so."

Privately, Kean told friends, "I have met one actor in this country, a young man named Edwin Forrest, who gives proofs of a decided genius for his profession, and will, I believe, rise to great eminence."

The season of 1825–1826 closed in Albany. Forrest finished full of hope and low in cash. When he heard that his manager, Charles Gilfert, would open the new Bowery Theatre in New York, he knew he must take his chances in Manhattan, even if that meant leaving his trunk with his landlady as security for back rent.

Edwin Forrest arrived in New York in the summer of 1826, when horsepower was the only practical transportation. That great city was thronged with steeds and high-stepping pedestrians. Five-story "horse hotels" were being projected by architects as the only possible solution to congestion. This was a time of great progress and expansion. No wonder that construction of the opulent Bowery Theatre, to become largest in the city after the Park, was far behind schedule. To make matters worse, Forrest found no work during that hot summer and became thoroughly disgusted.

He had grown used to the jangle of money in his pocket. While in New Orleans, he had joined the escapades of the wildest drinkers. When one friend, a riverboat captain and gambler, decided he had been crossed by the madam who operated a waterfront sporting house, Forrest helped him tie towropes to the establishment's pilings, and the captain pulled the rickety building right out into the muddy water with his boat.

In Albany, Forrest had frolicked in the streets with other players during the wee hours. Once he blocked a constable by reciting Shakespeare at the top of his lungs while his companions made good their escape. When he was haled into court, the judge caught him short with some Shakespeare of his own:

> What's the matter
> That you unlace your reputation thus,
> And spend your rich opinion for the name
> Of a night brawler? Give me answer to it!

The life of Gotham, even in 1826, was not kind to Forrest's purse. Soon broke, he scouted his friends. Jacob Woodhull, an actor in the Park Theatre company, tried to persuade him to appear in a benefit performance as Othello the Moor, Kean's role in the Albany production.

"I am obligated to Charles Gilfert, at the Bowery Theatre," Forrest explained. "I will be featured."

Woodhull must have pointed out that the Bowery stage of the moment consisted of several large stacks of boards. Yet Forrest realized that a poor showing in the benefit *Othello* might ruin his reputation. Gilfert, a fat Dutchman with a waddling gait, thought so too. Woodhull then offered Forrest a share in the gate receipts, and that did the trick.

The finesse of Edmund Kean's English acting style influenced Edwin Forrest
when he played Iago to Kean's Othello. Gravure by Gebbie & Husson, Co.,
Ltd., 1888

However, Forrest saw more than a chance at immediate cash. Should he triumph at the Park, he might go on to the Bowery with star billing, rather than to supporting roles.

Charles Gilfert crammed himself into a seat at the Park for the occasion. He sat dourly, expecting the worst. However, at first act's end, the man whose new Bowery Theatre could lift Forrest to stardom was applauding and stomping like everybody else.

For several performances as Othello, Forrest received $461, taking $400 to his debt-ridden mother. He wrote later, "The applause I had won before the foot-lights? Yes, it was most welcome and precious to me; but compared with this, it was nothing, less than nothing. Her fond and approving eyes seemed to sink into my very bones."

Precious to him as well were the words of reviewer Charles Durang: "Forrest entered with a calm mien and a dignified manner and took the center of the stage."

Promising . . . Edwin thought, the newspaper quivering in his hands.

"His youthful manly form—an expressive youthful face—"

Forget my youthfulness . . .

"A flashing hazel eye that foreshadowed vivid intellect—deportment and action naturally graceful and well costumed . . . at once struck like an electrical chord of harmony from the actor to the audience."

Praise heaven!

"I can only say that Forrest came upon us with all the genius—the spirit and power of the great Edmund Kean."

Incredible good fortune! And that with a leap in the air.

Gilfert made the most of his new man, billing him with tremendous publicity, paying him well, encouraged by critics who said that America had finally produced a great tragedian.

Forrest played the Bowery Theatre that season to packed houses of three thousand and standing room that paid the full price. In eleven particularly good evenings he pocketed more than $3,000 playing *Damon and Pythias, Julius Caesar, Othello,* and *King Lear.* Forrest soon adjusted to his success, and when Gilfert told him that the celebrated English actor William Macready would play a stand at the Park Theatre, they agreed that Forrest should make a run in opposition.

Forrest had the audacity to do plays that had actually been written especially for Macready. One of these, *William Tell,* was given with

Macready seated in the audience. The older man said Forrest showed promise, and that if he gave himself to severe study, he might become a first-rate actor—but that blinded by applause in low-priced theaters, he probably would not.

From other English sources, Forrest gathered that his lack of gentility was balanced by that robustness considered "American." He luxuriated in a lusty naturalism as the first American-grown star. The election of "Old Hickory" Andrew Jackson, in 1828, Forrest could point out, with a slam of his fist to the table, proved that a common-born man could rise to the Presidency.

Patriotic zeal in Forrest eventually bound him to Whitman, who said, "The United States themselves are essentially the greatest poem." Putting up $500 as a prize and appointing a committee to do the judging, the actor called for writers to submit tragedies in five acts in which the hero or principal character "shall be an aboriginal of this country."

The Indian was then a constant enemy on the near frontier; Black Hawk and his Sac and Fox warriors had not yet been driven across the Mississippi. Fascinated as he was by Indian custom, Forrest understood that in ennobling the enemy he ennobled Americans, whose bravery was being tested.

As one of the judges, Forrest appointed William Cullen Bryant, well-known poet and, like himself, an idealizer of "savages."

The winner was *Metamora; or, the Last of the Wampanoags,* a play based on the life of the real King Philip, Metacomet, by John Augustus Stone. It opened in 1829, full of exciting tableaux, splendid opportunities for displaying Forrest's muscular body, and stirring speeches such as the following:

"Our lands! Our nation's freedom! Or the grave!"

Metamora was a money-maker, its hero modeled on the sachem who had warred against New England settlers before the Revolution. Using the material he had absorbed during his stay with Push-ma-ta-ha, Forrest took off, declaiming with an energy most Indians had probably reserved for actual combat. One critic wrote, "Forrest's voice was tremendous in its sustained crescendo swell and crashing force of utterance . . . like the angry sea; as it reached its boiling, seething climax, in which the serpent hiss of hate was heard, at intervals amidst louder, deeper, hoarser tones, it was like the falls of Niagara."

In the next contest, Robert Montgomery Bird's *The Gladiator* was the

Forrest's months of living with the Indians prepared him for the part of *Metamora; or, the Last of the Wampanoags*. Steel engraving by Jas. Bannister, from a daguerreotype by Mathew Brady, 1877

Forrest took his performance of Spartacus in *The Gladiator* to Covent Garden in 1836, but was criticized for "a provincial flavor of the backwoods." Gravure by Gebbie & Co., 1887

winner. This play on the slave revolt in ancient Rome gave Forrest the role of Spartacus—again featuring naked muscle, violence, and harsh speeches about freedom. Throughout his lifetime these two roles were to be repeated hundreds of times, earning him hundreds of thousands of dollars. Their initial success was so great that, in 1834, Forrest elected to travel in England and Europe.

"The American Sensation" had been preceded abroad by his fame. In every circle he was welcomed for his vigor and good looks. If he lacked a certain polish, well, he *was* American, after all.

Edwin Forrest had not attended school past the age of ten, but he was a voracious reader, and he could be eloquent. However, he all too often would pack a conversation off in the direction he liked and knew best: stories of Indian pageantry, superstition, and war. When Forrest tired of his rustic "American" role, he would slip out to search for feminine companionship. After two years in England, France, Switzerland, Italy, and Russia, he returned eagerly to large American audiences. A new stage light had been invented—the *lime*light—used first in Scotland for surveying, because the sighter could make a "fix" at night over long distances. Forrest noted with interest how a torch of oxyhydrogen flame aimed at a block of calcium oxide, or lime, produced a brilliant white incandescence in the chemical. Placed in rows, these lights greatly enhanced his style as they shone on his legs, arms, and chest, grown thicker and more heavily corded with years of gymnastics.

Now the limelight turned him into a giant, every rouged smirk into a leer, each drawn sword into a lightning bolt.

Back in America, Forrest became even more daring in his method. He invented a dagger which, by releasing a trigger, spilled a pool of bloodred paint. His stage deaths, prolonged and agonizing, were demonstrations of titanic suffering, complete with death rattle. Gentler folk were known to bury their faces in their handkerchiefs. Faintings were not uncommon. But in the main, theatergoers crowed for more, and a standing joke went, "Wake me up when Forrest dies."

In the midst of renewed American acclaim, Edwin Forrest decided that he must return to England as an actor and take the London stage by storm. He would listen to no counterargument, so the tour of his American company was arranged, despite his being told that "George Washington never went to Europe to gain immortality, why should you?"

On October 17, 1836, Forrest opened at Covent Garden in *The*

Edwin Forrest in his prime. Engraved by D. Pound from a daguerreotype by Root of New York

Gladiator. As Spartacus, the half-clad rebel slave, he won comments from critics about his "thew and sinew," and remarks on "a provincial flavor of the backwoods."

The English had lost two American wars and a rich colony. They were not about to lose this war of the stage.

There *were* good reviews: "The first tragedian of the age." "Heart-thrilling." "A powerful and original actor."

The opposition stirred. William Macready, mature, controlled, and sophisticated in his Hamlet or Richard III, was a dominant figure of the London stage. His good friend, John Forster, critic for the London *Examiner,* was faced with the problem.

"Deal liberally and kindly," Macready wrote wisely to the critic, realizing that because he and Forster were linked by the public, too sudden an attack would cause suspicion. But in his diary, Macready admitted that it would be "shallow hypocrisy" to say that bad notices about Forrest worried him.

Forster had a mind of his own. Of Spartacus he said, "A few real gladiators at an English supper-table" would be as proper as "such a succession of scenes in an English theatre."

Macready cautioned Forster again; he responded by writing of Forrest that it took "more skill to finger and stop an instrument than to blow it."

Theatrical groups organized teas and dinners to have a close look at the American. Macready, of course, was usually there. At one function, the English rival raised a toast, explaining that "no one extended the hand of welcome to him more fervently or sincerely than myself."

Not many weeks after this toast was drunk, Forster ripped into Forrest's Richard III: "A savage newly caught from out of the American woods."

Forrest turned his back; he was in love. The parents of lovely Catherine Sinclair lived with their eighteen-year-old daughter in England, but John Sinclair had come from Scotland, the native land of Forrest's father. He had served in the Argyleshire militia and was a famous singer of Scottish ballads. Mrs. Sinclair had been an actress. Both had performed in America. After a quarrel over Catherine's dowry, Forrest brought his bride home to meet his mother in Philadelphia.

Edwin Forrest was ecstatically happy. He and Catherine traveled four thousand miles overland while he gave 158 performances and earned $33,956 during their first season together.

On June 27, 1839, he wrote his mother from Harrisburg: "We expected to be with you in Philadelphia today but have been prevented by the entrance into this breathing world of a little girl. Catherine is doing very well and begs to be remembered to the family."

The premature child died a few weeks later.

When Edwin learned that William Macready was coming to America to contest him on his own ground, the grieving father met him with understandable bitterness.

Forrest changed his schedule in order to match Macready, Hamlet for Hamlet, in Philadelphia. One writer reported that you had a choice between "Native Americanism" and "Foreignism." Forrest was called "a rough jewel of the first water; Macready a paste gem, polished and set off with every counterfeit gleam art could lend. The fire of the American commands honest throbs and tears; the icy glitter of the Englishman, dainty clappings of kid gloves."

Perhaps Edwin was overly encouraged. A year later, against all advice, he again played London, opening in *Othello*. Forster, the critic and Macready's friend, was waiting.

"The grin of a wolf showing his fangs," he said of Forrest's Othello. His portrayal of Macbeth was "a comic act."

Forrest could take such abuse, but when one performance of *Othello* was met by tittering and hissing, repeatedly from the same section of the audience, he became convinced that there was a Macready claque.

Forrest kept his peace, and then one night in October, 1845, when Macready was playing Hamlet at the Theatre Royal, Edinburgh, the American appeared close above the stage in a private box.

At a particularly sensitive moment in the performance, Forrest hissed. The sound was referred to by witnesses as the hiss of a steam engine. Macready looked up to see the glaring face of his rival. Without show of emotion, he continued the play. But later, in theatrical circles, he attacked Forrest with fire unexpected in a man fifty-eight years of age.

For two years the battle raged.

In print, Forrest said, "Clapping the hands and hissing are two legitimate modes of evincing approbation and disapprobation in the theatre, one expressive of approval, the other of disapproval. The latter is a salutary and wholesome corrective of abuses of the stage. A fellow actor has as much right to this as anyone else."

Macready returned to America to continue the feud. Appearing in

Forrest's Philadelphia, he told his audience that, on his sacred honor, he had never been impolite to an American actor, but that he had been hissed in public by an American. Next day, Forrest published a notice in the *Ledger* referring to a pussy-footing Englishman, and wondering why this man did not charge him openly, "for I did it, and publicly avowed it. . . . I assert and solemnly believe that Mr. Macready connived with his friends to hiss me . . . many months before . . . at Edinburgh. . . . Pah!"

Talk of the rivalry dominated stage life in both countries; partisans of Macready on both sides of the Atlantic tended to be in the minority and of the upper classes. The American appealed to working men.

Neither faction, however, was prepared for the terrible denouement to this feud, which occurred in New York, in the spring of 1849.

Macready had been scheduled to appear at the Astor Place Opera House in *Macbeth*.

Forrest had opened well at the Broadway and would continue.

The chief of police, discovering that, as the papers put it, "the excitement among the theatre-going people has been rising to fever heat," stationed deputies at the doors to the Opera House.

Moderates suggested that Forrest withdraw temporarily from competition to prevent trouble. That he was in no mood to comply is not surprising. His bitterness had other sources: the weakening of his marriage, due to his absences and the death of other children, four in all; the recent death of his mother; and above all, an almost paranoid conviction that his wife had been unfaithful.

On the eve of his confrontation with Macready, he and Catherine parted. Would he withdraw until this "fever heat" in the public subsided? Macready be damned. Two Macbeths strode two stages that evening, May 8, 1849.

Walt Whitman had said once that Macready "touched the heart, the soul, the feelings, the inner blood and nerves of the audience." But Whitman spoke of calmer evenings. This evening, Forrest's furious declamation was met with hurrahs, Macready's subtlety with a shower of eggs and vegetables.

Macready refused to leave the stage. Splotched and unheard, he continued the part in pantomime. Roughnecks tore up chairs and hurled them at an actor in danger of losing his life. Terrified, he at last fled the theater.

There was no question but that someone had planned the demonstration, for when Macready had gone, a member of the mob jumped onstage with a banner lettered, "Macready has left the theater."

"Three groans for the English bulldog," came the reply.

The news filtered to Forrest between acts. He had won. When he finished his show, he found the city in an uproar.

However, an anti-Forrest faction was showing new strength. *His* supporters were labeled "unwashed." Forty-seven leading New Yorkers, headed by Herman Melville and Washington Irving, confronted Macready as he packed, begging him to grant another performance. Macready agreed to appear on the night of May 10.

Before the performance began, two hundred police were stationed at strategic points inside the Astor Place Opera House. Fifty more stood in Eighth Street. Two hundred soldiers of the Seventh Regiment and two troops of cavalry lurked nearby.

When the hall opened, eighteen hundred spectators surged inside; thousands remained milling around in Astor Place.

Between scenes, runners brought Forrest the news that Macready's entrance had been met by boos and catcalls, that the police had arrested ringleaders, and that a plank had been thrown from the balcony, a chandelier smashed by stones.

That the mob inside had notified the mob outside to act against the police, and that police behind street barricades were heavily bombarded with stones.

That the police had been driven to cover inside the theater by the mob. And that cavalry called into action to clear the square had been taunted and stoned.

The military were pinned against the walls of the theater.

An order was given to fire over the heads of the rioters, which was done, with little effect. The order was given to fire into their legs; a dozen rioters fell screaming. The mob surged toward the soldiers, swinging sticks and throwing stones dead level. The infantry fired again, and again.

Twenty-two people were killed!

3
The Challenged

"THIS BLOOD," wrote Edwin Forrest in a steady hand, "will rest on the heads of the Committee who insisted that Macready should perform in despite of the known wishes of the people to the contrary." He had discharged his conscience, and without much reluctance acknowledged the stream of congratulatory messages and telegrams that flowed in.

Forrest continued to perform without difficulty. When he could, however, he withdrew to Fonthill, a precarious, turreted "castle" he had built for Catherine overlooking the Hudson north of New York City. Closeted there in the gardener's cottage or later in the main house, he brooded about his dead mother, his ruined marriage, and the sons and daughters who had never held his hand.

But he did not brood over the souls of twenty-two shot dead in Astor Place.

Forrest, in fact, grew increasingly strange, and with time the stone halls of Fonthill echoed a new Lear.

Gradually, the great actor had become more interested in the mad king of Shakespeare's most moving play. Obsessed by this role as never before, Forrest took to stopping at insane asylums while traveling from one engagement to another to inquire about inmates possessing King Lear's general characteristics.

Through friends, he visted John Rush in a Philadelphia asylum and in him found an ideal model. John, the son of Dr. Benjamin Rush, father of American psychiatry, had years earlier killed a friend after a quarrel and had become insane.

As Forrest grew older and more embittered, he himself, inhabitant of a self-designed castle, began to resemble the Lear he had studied so deeply.

After fighting his wife in the courts with increasing rancor, Forrest lost

The embittered Forrest began to merge his personality with the Lear he played so movingly. Gravure by Gebbie & Husson Co., Ltd., 1887

a state supreme court decision. Faced with alimony, he sold Fonthill and other real estate, consolidated his resources, and retired from the theater, encouraged in that direction by an attack of gout that kept him bedridden for months.

Sciatica and rheumatism followed at intervals. In time, he was to lose the use of his right arm, walk with difficulty, and be in continual pain. But for all his irascibility in the past, Forrest now, as his shadow lengthened, showed courage bordering on the superhuman.

Sporadically, he emerged from retirement with plans for a new career. During the Civil War he became active and agreed to appear at Ford's Theatre, Washington, D.C.

During his time in Washington, sciatica struck, sending thunderbolts of pain through his legs. Each day he remained in bed, motionless; each night he forced himself to go onstage.

News that on January 18, 1865, Abraham Lincoln would attend his performance of *Jack Cade* inspired in Forrest some of his old energy; he would play the rigorous role to the hilt for a President who could appreciate this tale of revolt among English bondsmen and the winning of rights from nobility.

Another actor noted Lincoln's scheduled appearance with interest— John Wilkes Booth, whose accomplices planned to abduct the President on that occasion.

Lincoln did not appear.

By March, sun, pills, and ointments had reduced Forrest's pain. He accepted an engagement for Niblo's Garden, New York City, in April.

Sunday, April 9, the bells of the city rang in an endless toll; the telegraph had brought news of Lee's surrender to Grant at Appomattox. Forrest returned to his engagement at Niblo's Garden, despite a hugely inflamed right leg. The audience, distracted by the war news, seemed indifferent. On Friday, April 14, in great pain, Forrest shambled through *Othello*. In Washington, Lincoln, comfortable in his rocking chair in a box at Ford's Theatre, watched Laura Keene in *Our American Cousin*.

Forrest was in his room at the Metropolitan Hotel, bathing his leg, when his friend John McCullough rushed in.

"Wilkes Booth has shot Lincoln," he shouted. "I don't believe it, I don't believe it!"

"Well, I do," growled Forrest. "All those damned Booths are crazy."

The Booths had been unshakable. Junius Brutus Booth, an expatriate

Englishman, had dogged Forrest on the American stage, using a style similar to his and Kean's, yet they had become friends. J. B. named his son, Edwin, after Forrest. Now Edwin, at thirty two, was breaking records Forrest had set in every theater in the East. To top it off, Edwin's young brother, John Wilkes, by this insane murder, had brought the public down on the profession.

As he grew older, Forrest began to take Edwin's success less and less smoothly; this young man was forcing him, old and paralyzed, from the stage. Against Booth, Forrest fought his final popularity contest, traveling from coast to coast to every major city, despite his infirmities.

Edwin Booth's style was prophetic in its gentle naturalness. Delicate and brooding, Booth made the ideal Hamlet. Walt Whitman reacted scornfully to this "still, small voice," remembering Forrest's broad sweep and thundering style.

To meet public demand, Booth used extravagant stage sets. Forrest, from the audience, accused him one night of conducting a scenery painter's drama. Invited to play Iago to Booth's Othello, Forrest resoundingly refused. In Philadelphia, he visited the Walnut Street Theatre, where the stage manager was setting up scenery for Booth's *Hamlet.*

"I never needed these contraptions," stormed Forrest, "and neither did his father." Because of Forrest's anger and influence, the manager destroyed the scenery.

Again and again, Forrest toured the "provinces" as his pull in major cities waned. Illness dogged him. His stage manager operated under instructions to tell the other actors never to touch Forrest's feet or right arm. Some evenings he was so paralyzed that his sword had to be strapped to his arm before the mock duel.

Gone were the days when he terrified audiences by driving his sword into a column at stage left as he exited, leaving it quivering. Once in Boston an Englishman had run from the theater screaming, "The damned brute is going to chop down the house!"

Now he dueled in slow motion.

Damon and Pythias called for a three-foot leap from a platform which, season by season, had been lowered, until, with a pathetic hop, the half-crippled actor let himself down a height of three inches. One night he was so lame that the stage carpenter simply lay down two flat boards.

Forrest gazed pitifully at the structure.

"I have struck this role from my repertoire," he sighed.

Not that he had given up by any means. In his last brutal tour he traveled 8,000 miles and gave 156 performances without a lapse, easily outdoing two veterans known for long careers—Fanny Kemble and David Garrick.

An unfavorable critic, visiting Forrest, found him "bent over like a wounded lion about to spring, his disabled arm held up like a massive paw . . . the veins in his neck tied in knots . . . hissing as of lava issuing from his lips."

After several performances his voice might be reduced to a whisper. His audiences became thinner and thinner. Fabulous entertainments, in addition to Edwin Booth, drew them away—plays like *The Black Crook*, involving a mad chemist and dozens of scantily clothed maidens, and *Under the Gaslight* in which a villain (for the first time) tied the heroine to the railroad tracks. In this and other melodramas the gorgeous and busty damsel narrowly avoided death; clever sets and sound effects magnified the horror.

Forrest struggled on, reduced at times to mere readings of his famous parts; he spoke leaning on a lectern.

But in what remained, his Lear stood. This king of the stage, toward the end, on strong nights, seemed completely to embody that role.

Eleanor Ruggles has so perfectly captured this that her words bear repeating:

"He had played King Lear in New York, the last engagement of his life there, with poor support and dingy settings, yet never had he acted the part more movingly. As he slowly advanced onstage, inclining his head to the faint applause from the half-filled benches, he made such a figure of ruined majesty that the handful of spectators could hardly keep their tears back. The critics no longer scoffed at him. . . . After one neglected performance a reporter cried to him, 'Mr. Forrest, I never in my life saw you play Lear so well as you did tonight!'

"The old actor rose. He drew himself up. '*Play* Lear?' he retorted. 'What do you mean, sir? I do not *play* Lear. I *play* Hamlet, Richard, Shylock, if you please, but by God, sir, I *am* Lear!' "

Forrest did not go down easily. He soaked in tubs. He had special stoves installed in dressing rooms. He saw a succession of doctors, used steam to 215 degrees, visited hot springs and cold springs. He believed in the healing power of shock and in the coldest weather plunged outdoors stark naked, then returned to his hot water. He was never without his dumbbells, with which he exercised regularly, sometimes if only by raising them briefly from the floor.

In his sixty-sixth year, Forrest gave up the readings as a "damned nuisance." Abed, he awaited the return of strength; when it came, he would launch himself on a regular tour.

The morning of December 12, 1872, his servant, Katie, carrying his breakfast, opened the door to find him groaning and writhing. He could not speak, but his eyes plainly showed despair. In minutes he was dead.

He had died outside the tradition of his famous tragic death scenes— without words, without the gargle and gasp. If his Metamora or his Hamlet had, in their last moments, made the theater tremble, now the bed sheets barely quivered.

"He gave to his children, the public, all he had," one critic had said toward the end, "and now they have deserted him. They have crowned a new King, Edwin Booth, before whom they bow."

4
Junius Brutus Booth

THE PLAYBILL for the Winter Garden Theatre, New York, announced *Julius Caesar* for November 25, 1864, to be performed by "the three sons of the great Booth—Junius Brutus, Edwin, and John Wilkes."

"The great Booth" had been Junius Brutus Booth, Sr., a most unusual father. Now his widow watched her sons together, proud to the point of tears, for they had never been seen side by side on the stage.

When the play ended (Edwin played Brutus; John Wilkes, Marc Anthony, and J. B., Cassius), they bowed toward their mother. In this evening of triumph, Mary Anne Booth found her dream fulfilled. During the Civil War, John had been acting in the South, acclaimed by audiences. Junius, Jr., had succeeded on the western circuit, and Edwin had won the praise of sophisticated eastern audiences and critics. Now here they were together before her, bowing, smiling—together perhaps for the last time, she sensed, knowing the intensity of John's feelings about the South.

Ovation thundered on ovation. She must have listened, this woman almost old, with the queer sensation one has of time stopped when sitting upon the rocks beside a great ocean surf, awed by the roar. So this audience roared, having to itself three sons of the great Booth.

A mother's eyes were moist with tears. A handkerchief was raised. A half smile. *How Edwin resembled his father! Was that why she preferred John Wilkes, or was he more handsome? Certainly their father had been the most difficult of the Booth men. He had been difficult from the start. Not that Edwin was difficult. But Junius, oh, that Junius, oh, dear!*

She was a poor girl, from Reading, in England. Although she could read in those days so long ago, she had had to be content with selling flowers in the Bow Street Market outside Covent Garden, London, to get along.

At Covent Garden, Mary Anne had watched a well-cut, handsome young actor come and go. His name was Junius Booth, said the handbills, and he was the principal threat to the great Edmund Kean, tiger of the London stage. One night when Booth bought violets, their eyes met. Next night, having spent a good share of her savings, she found herself in a theater seat, all glow and gooseflesh, as the curtain rose on *King Lear*.

After the show Booth again bought violets.

"My," she said, "were *you* really that little old man?"

The married Booth probably thought twice before asking Mary Anne Holmes to join him for refreshment in a nearby tavern. However, he did not live to regret his decision. He found in simple-seeming Mary Anne complex depth of feeling. Arranging to see her regularly, he took her to the Channel islands. He had fallen in love.

Booth kept nothing from his sweetheart. He had fought hard for his success, he told her; fought against the resistance of his father, Richard Booth, an important lawyer who had insisted that he attend the best schools. Well, he had thrown that over. He had seen and acted in plays in school, and it was acting for *him,* so he had joined a troop of wandering players. They found him a trifle short and bowlegged, but they let him perform. Sleeping in fields and barns, they often begged for food. Yes, it had been hard. Now on the verge of professional permanence, he found life again discouraging, for he was married to a woman who meant little or nothing to him. She was Adelaide, the daughter of an innkeeper who, Booth said, had lodged him during a tour in Brussels, Belgium, and forced him to wed his daughter.

Junius could well remember the hopelessness of that situation. Summoning up all his cleverness, he had written to his father, asking for money on the pretense of setting himself up in the jewelry business:

F. A. Jones, a very respectable man who is by business a jeweller and who has brought over with him on speculation several articles in that line, has been advised to set up in business here, and he, on account of my knowledge of the language in which I have made wonderful progress . . . has kindly offered to instruct me . . . if I can get some things to work upon which must be bought here and we then would open a shop for the sale of jewellery. Now in order to do this it is necessary to have the *Sinews* of every enterprise, *Money* which if it please you venture, as I intend quitting the stage in toto. I find it a life of so much idleness and care too, and no money to be got at it, that if I can establish myself in

the line aforesaid, I will strive every nerve to succeed in it and endeavor
to become a respectable member of society. The theatrical mania that
caged within me begins to die away, I perceive.

How Mary Anne laughed as he recited this past cleverness. Give up
the stage? Never. He had sought money to help himself and dull Adelaide
into some sort of solution. Unheeded, he and the girl had returned to
London, he told Mary Anne, and there they were married. A baby girl
was born. Junius himself was soon invited to challenge the famous Edmund Kean on the stage—causing near riots among the public through
their rivalry. With repeated performances in the important cities came
fame. Then his little daughter suddenly died.

Mary Anne's eyes turned down.

Nothing had glowed for him, he said, as brightly as the love he and
Mary Anne now felt.

Mary Anne's face revealed her conflict. He seemed to love her, to want
her, despite his other ties. *Yes, he did love her.* She decided to be completely honest with him. She said softly one evening, "I am going to have
a baby."

Booth acted at once. Edmund Kean was breathing down his neck, a
rivalry dangerous to both actors; Mary Anne must be protected. Reports
of eager American audiences had reached his ears. They soon set sail.

Junius had been strongly influenced by his father to love the new country. Richard Booth, as a boy, had run away to fight in the Revolution on
the American side, but was hauled back by authorities. He kept a portrait
of General Washington in his house, and ordered all visitors to remove
their hats as they passed before it. Junius in emigrating fulfilled his father's
dream. He informed Adelaide of his plan to perform in America, promising to send money for their young son—a promise he kept. About Mary
Anne he told her nothing. So with the slate wiped skillfully clean, Junius
and Mary Anne unpacked in America, brimming with love and optimism.

A difficult land this actor found: cities far apart, travel brutally grinding as rough coaches and wagons pitched over rutted roads.

Charles Gilfert, who helped Edwin Forrest in New York six years later,
was manager in 1820 of the National Theatre in Richmond, Virginia,
and readily booked the English success in *Richard III*. Junius, who arrived after a fifteen-mile walk precipitated by a wagon breakdown, di-

sheveled and looking shorter than usual, was taken for a boy come in to watch rehearsal.

Onstage, his bearing erased this illusion. He strutted, he commanded, he soared. And that *voice*. It dusted the seats in the back row. Even Gilfert applauded.

But there was something dismaying about this young Booth, a strange carelessness, a wandering of the mind. During his early tours it was noticed that he seemed to stumble absentmindedly through portions of a play, bursting into eloquence during grander speeches. Where did his agile mind stray?

Whatever the infirmity, his drinking probably speeded the change— that and hard, hard work, and then tragedy.

He was a remarkably gentle person, with two sides to his nature, one that flared, as he grew older, toward maniacal, highly imaginative expression, and another side that was artistic, soulful, tender. Onstage, particularly in acting Shakespeare, poetry of tongue and action were joined. These sides, bound together on the stage, divided in the man when he was set free from a script. To act was the cure for some terrifying internal schism.

Mary Anne had given birth to a healthy boy, Junius Brutus Booth, Jr. She did her best to manage while her husband toured. Rosalie, Elizabeth, Henry Byron, Frederick, and Mary Anne arrived in short order. Booth established them on a small farm near Bel Air, Maryland; he became a gentleman farmer in the off season.

Though Booth traveled far and wide, his heart remained at home. Separations were acutely painful for him.

"My love for you is still undiminished," he wrote. "Take care of your Health & don't be dull or fretting. . . . God bless you dear Wife."

Except for incidental problems, the messages that reached Junius during his road tours were of routine good wishes and long-suffering love. Booth was ill prepared when at Richmond, Virginia, he broke the seal of a letter informing him that his four-year-old son, Frederick, was desperately sick with scarlet fever. Calling for a horse, Booth rode to Maryland at top speed, but found the child dead. Brooding, he turned back toward Richmond. The show would go on.

News that his little girl, Elizabeth, was sick overtook him on his journey. She saw her father again shortly before she died.

Philadelphia Theatre.

The Doors will be opened at a quarter past 5, and the Curtain rise at precisely a quarter past 6 o'clock, until further notice.

Last Night of Mr. Booth's Engagement.

Friday Evening, Dec. 26, 1823,

Will be presented Maturin's admired Tragedy of

BERTRAM;

Or, the Castle of St. Aldobrand.

Bertram, (first time here)	Mr. BOOTH.	First Robber,		Mr. JOHNSTON.
St. Aldobrand,	Mr. DARLEY.	Second Robber,		Mr. BIGNALL.
Prior of St. Anselm,	Mr. WHEATLY.	Page,		Miss HATHWELL.
First Monk,	Mr. HATHWELL.	Child,		Miss H. HATHWELL
Second Monk,	Mr. SCRIVENER.	Imogene,		Mrs. WOOD.
Third Monk,	Mr. GREENE.	Clotilda,		Mrs. GREENE.
Hugo,	Mr. MURRAY.	Teresa,		Mrs. MURRAY

Knights, Monks, Soldiers, Banditti, &c.

After which, the Musical Drama of

The Libertine.

Written by the Author of Rob Roy, &c.

And performed in London, and New York, with unbounded applause. The Music from Mozart's celebrated Opera of Don Giovanni, and adapted to the English Stage by Bishop.

Don Juan,	Mr. WALLACK.	Leporello,		Mr. JEFFERSON.
Don Pedro,	Mr. HATHWELL.	Masetto,		Mr. DARLEY.
Don Octavio,	Mr. JOHNSTON.	Lopez,		Mr. GREENE.

Peasants—Serenaders—Female Masqueraders, &c. &c.

Donna Elvira,	Mrs. ANDERSON.	Maria,		Mrs. JEFFERSON.
Donna Leonora,	Mrs. C. DURANG.	Zerlina,		Mrs. BURKE.

Dæmons—Attendants—Officers, &c.

SCENE FIRST,
The Garden of DON PEDRO'S House at Seville—
Part of the Mansion.
SCENE FIFTH,

Luxuriant Gardens, and a distant View.

Preparations for a Fete—at the Side, a Summer House, &c
IN THIS SCENE,

A RUSTIC BALLET,

BY THE CHARACTERS,
Principal parts by Mrs. WALLACK & Miss HATHWELL, &
ACT SECOND,

A Cemetry, near Seville,

Various Tombs and Memorials—in the centre, a

Large Equestrian Statue,

Erected to the memory of the late commandant.—SCENE 2d.

A HALL AND BANQUET.

THE SCENE CHANGES TO A

BURNING CAVERN.

With Hideous Monsters, breathing Flames, &c.—Furies seize the Libertine. who at length sinks, pursued through every part of the Scene, till he is seized, and enfolded by

A MONSTROUS SERPENT.

On Saturday, (for the first time here) a new Historical Drama, called

Joan of Arc; or, the Maid of Orleans.

With New Dresses, &c.

Booth is featured in a varied program on this original playbill

Booth's sensitive personality crumbled. Mary Anne nursed him back to health; again he took the road. Again he was called back. Another little child, named Mary Anne for her mother, had suddenly died of a contagious disease.

Booth arrived at the doorway of his dear home in a blizzard to find it encrusted in frozen black crepe paper, tattered by the storm, crackling in the wind. Booth pounded, and they let him in. Raging, he called his field hands, and ordered them to the graveyard with picks and shovels. He would have his Mary Anne.

She was brought into the warm house. For hours, he crouched over her, praying to God for a miracle. In the morning he turned from the lifeless form, walked haggardly to the barn, where he laboriously fitted his shoes with lead soles, filled them with dried peas, and to do penance for his guilt, set off down the highway. He arrived at Washington, D.C., late the following night, exhausted and quiet. He had come thirty-nine miles, and at the inn, peculiarly calm, he called for grog and a tub to soak his feet.

Junius Booth returned to the stage. Periodically, his resolve weakened, and fortified with drink, he berated his audiences. One time he appeared at the top of a stepladder crowing like a cock. He played *Julius Caesar* standing on tiptoe. He did *The Merchant of Venice* once in a whisper. On another occasion he failed to appear for the second act; they found him blocks away heaving on the hand pumps of a fire engine, in full Shylock costume.

At one time, Junius renounced his profession entirely. He filed application for the post of keeper of the Cape Hatteras lighthouse. He would give his Shakespeare to the waves—more appreciative, he said, than the stinking pit crowd, with "their ears filled with cobwebs, cockroaches and the babble of each other's voices." Booth's manager with difficulty blocked Booth's desertion of the stage.

Later, Booth developed an inordinate love of animals, filling his letters with instructions that none of the pigs be slaughtered, and that his dog, Boatswain, "should have a run once or twice every day and his tub of water." He had become a vegetarian, he told everyone firmly, because the souls of people transmigrated into the bodies of animals at death. He refused to kill any living thing; you never knew which poor fellow had become a chicken, duck, or lamb. His farm was overrun by untouchable livestock. Hogs ran wild while the Booths bought bacon.

Copperhead snakes lolled in luxury, untroubled by sticks or guns. One was injured by the plow. Booth put it upon cloths in Mary Anne's hatbox to get well. She told a neighbor, "For three days that fearful reptile occupied our parlor!"

Junius Booth's strangeness did not lessen with the arrival of more children. His ways remained as odd, and to make matters worse, he drank longer and harder with the years. When he was rational and sober, he was a fine father. He read good books, learned new languages, and played his stage roles flawlessly—although he made his major speeches in a somewhat ear-piercing style.

His children mimicked him, wore his costumes—plumed hats, capes, swords. Booth addressed them by their titles—kings, queens, lords, and ladies. They were otherwise known as Rosalie, Henry Byron, Edwin Thomas, Asia, Joseph Adrian, and John Wilkes, the last—and of course, Junius Brutus Booth, Jr., the eldest, born before they moved to the farm.

Rosalie was a little odd, remaining content to help with the housework. Junius, Jr., solid, assertive, stable, and eager, was persuaded by his father to study surgery, but gave it up for acting. Asia was exciting, imaginative, though subject to spells of sulking and jealousy. Joseph seemed to have a lot of his father's instability. He was to bungle acting, become a physician, then for years to loll in indecision over whether to practice medicine or not.

John Wilkes was the baby of the family. Handsome, electric, aggressive, he fascinated everyone, and got badly spoiled in the process. Mary Anne doted on him, and told again and again how, while she was nursing him beside the fireplace one evening, she had prayed for a message about his future. Then, she claimed, the fire flew up into the form of an arm. John Wilkes rode roughshod over the hillsides brandishing a Mexican War saber. His mother smothered him with affection, promised that he would one day wear his father's costumes and fill his roles.

Edwin Booth was almost overlooked. Taciturn, often somber, he was overshadowed by the others, particularly Johnny. This was a household in which a shy boy could easily be lost. He never knew what to expect. One day his father issued invitations to neighboring farmers announcing the funeral of a friend. They arrived, a skeptical and tolerant lot, to find themselves at the funeral of Booth's pet pony, Peacock. Of course, the Booth children all stood solemnly by, their best collars under their chins and their hats in hand. Edwin and John Wilkes hoped at such times that

Onstage, Booth was a whole man and a true artist. In private he was increasingly erratic and irrational. Gravure by Gebbie & Husson Co., Ltd., 1887

their father was not quite serious, despite the macabre nature of the situation. Doubt about his intentions was dispelled when they were in Bel Air and saw him stop a stranger and, offering a scrap of tanned hide from his pocket, demand, "What animal is this, eh?" The perplexed fellow shook his head.

"That's a *man's* hide," Booth said in this often-repeated demonstration. "We animals are all alike."

The farm was not an unpleasant place—a log cabin nestling in small fields against a backdrop of dense forest was later replaced by a large house. At home, Mary Anne stood between gentle Edwin and the other children, and she protected him from their father during his gloomier or more violent moods. Edwin's quietness calmed his father at times.

Junius' troubles on tour increased. In Philadelphia, to publicize newly permitted Sunday performances, he rode through town in his Hamlet costume while people were walking to church. "Ladies and gentlemen," he shouted, "I intend to perform *Hamlet* tonight, and a good play is worth forty sermons." He closed with a bawdy Lincolnshire drinking song. The theater had to shut down immediately to avoid serious retaliation.

This sort of news wore on Mary Anne. One evening at supper she suggested, "Why don't you and Edwin tour together?" All looked up, startled; Teddy, as they called him at thirteen, was in the midst of his schooling.

"I will not have him an actor!" his father announced. "He will become a cabinetmaker, a good trade, using his hands and his brain. Keep him out of trouble." He grumbled while he drank his soup. He grumbled that evening and the next day, but it was no use. He had turned fifty and felt fifty, not a pleasant age for a man of his profession, forced to tour a rough countryside, earning money for the repertory companies in the cities along the route.

The open road called to Edwin's young mind, filled with stories of his father's adventures, carefully laundered. It offered an escape from the schoolroom, from the dull Latin and Greek of those formal days, and from violin lessons.

Edwin's eagerness met Junius' reluctance. What need had he of a nursemaid? Mary Anne talked to him carefully, and in time something of her concern softened his resistance. Yes, be damned, Teddy could trot along behind—but no acting, no acting of any sort. That must be a promise. So off they went.

Edwin Booth had seen his father act before, of course, but surprise would follow surprise in the reality of backstage life. For mathematics, violin lessons, and romps and rides in the open fields, he exchanged the odor of greasepaint, well-worn wigs and costumes, the shouting and clatter of rehearsals, and the scrape of scenery. In this milieu he utterly lost himself.

Wherever he went his father was the respected, the deferred to, the center of attention. He had never admired his father more.

Sitting in the wings, he listened to Junius intone the famous lines. Sometimes he sat beneath the stage on dusty rolls of canvas, and the stamp of feet above, sending fine wisps of dust upon his face, told him Hamlet was dueling to the death and soon must die.

Timidly at first, later with great zeal, Edwin mouthed the lines that drifted muffled to his ears, learning them word for word.

His father attacked his roles in a curious way. Almost coasting through dull sections, he braced for the rousing speeches that audiences loved the most. Edwin Forrest used the same technique.

"How will I ever make an actor?" Edwin asked once. "I'll never shout like that. I'm too weak."

"Never an actor," Booth swore. "A cabinetmaker. I've got to get you out of this life; I shall apprentice you to the next carpenter I meet. Now your books. Where are your books? Your mother insisted you bring them, so you will use them *now*."

Edwin made motions of studying. He deceived no one. Friends and fans came backstage to talk and fool after the show, and Edwin, shy and good-looking, was swallowed up, Latin forgotten.

He exchanged the violin for a banjo, played songs at parties that show people gave. Edwin Forrest came to admire his namesake, danced many a jig to the strumming, then sank exhausted in a chair.

"You have my name," he said, "but, my boy, you don't want my legs too. They've given out."

In this happy life, the years passed, six of them, and Edwin became a man. At sixteen he had been billed in his first minor part, in *Richard III*, as a messenger from the field of battle.

"How did you come?" demanded Junius.

"At high speed, on horseback," said Edwin.

"Then where are your spurs?"

"I haven't any," he said.

"Well, then, wear mine."

Edwin flushed. His spine tingled. For months his interest had been damned and discouraged; now he felt that his father might help him succeed in the profession he claimed he loathed.

Edwin appeared more and more frequently, often as Cassio to Junius' Iago, in *Othello.* The elder Booth, asked by reporters on whose shoulders his mantle would fall, placed his hand on his son's head. He had to reach up to do it.

At first the young man was billed as "Master Edwin Booth." Within a year, he was billed in full support as Edwin Booth. In April, 1851, his father fell ill, and Edwin was forced to take his role as Richard III. He was eighteen. The audience liked him. His voice was light, his stage business clumsy, but he was a new *Booth,* and they loved it.

Junius Brutus and Edwin then set sail for California to try their skill in the theaters of the gold-rush towns. The long voyage tired the father, and the hurly-burly of the wide-open towns was more than he could take. Edwin thrived.

"I'm going home," Junius announced to his son. "I am leaving the road." At fifty-six he was an old man.

He played New Orleans on the way, six days at the St. Charles, in *The Iron Chest* and in a comedy called *Review; or, the Wag of Windsor.* Then he boarded the steamer *J. S. Chenoweth* headed north for Cincinnati. There was no doctor aboard.

Two days out, he developed typhoid fever. He complained to no one; Booth had never been a complainer.

Five days out, he died.

Mary Anne claimed his body in Cincinnati. His had been a strange hard life and it was over.

He was laid out in the house in Baltimore, a bust of Shakespeare at his head. Actors throughout the nation wore black armbands, some even as they performed.

When Edwin heard the news, he sobbed, "I ought to have gone with him."

Senator Rufus Choate said, "What, Booth dead? Then there are no more actors!"

But of Booths there were two who would yet make their mark.

5

Brothers

THEY HAD HEARD that Edwin might come by nightfall, and they had been half in the yard, half in the house most of the afternoon. Now the cry went up, for at a distance some dust rose from a rain-wet roadway dried by clearing skies. Soon the thud of hoofs in scrambled beat told of a team rather than a single rider.

Mary Anne went down to the yard, wringing her hands. John Wilkes stood straight nearby, talking rapidly, and repeating, "Well, well, well," and waving his arms. *I've grown,* he thought. *I'm taller—I must be taller by now than my brother. We will see about it. After all, I am eighteen.*

John was very good-looking and ambitious. He had already debuted in Baltimore as the Earl of Richmond in *Richard III,* but was poorly received. He had told his schoolmates, "Fame! I must have fame!" Everyone seemed sure he would.

As Edwin's coach neared, John Wilkes grew more nervous. Edwin Booth had played in San Francisco opposite Catherine Sinclair, the former wife of Forrest, from whom she had won a divorce. Edwin had seasoned himself in small camp theaters from one end of the mining country to the other. Edwin had, his letters said, sailed to Australia, to successes opposite a rising feminine star, Laura Keene. What of that, though? He, Johnny, was the ascendant one; he felt it in his bones.

So when Edwin unlimbered from his carriage, red-eyed and weary, John Wilkes confidently embraced him after their mother had finished her hugs and weeping.

"My God," said Edwin, "look at the man of you!"

"You're the big one, Ted," said John.

"No, Johnny, you're the good-looking gentleman. They'll see you on the boards, eh? Come now, let's go in and all have the news, and I've presents for everyone."

But in the house Edwin fell still, for there were things here of his father's that subdued him; he had not been home since Junius' death. It was a new brick farmhouse, half finished when he had left, and now complete. Silent in his father's chair, Edwin leafed a text of his father's *Hamlet* filled with notes on the playing.

John Wilkes watched, wondering again who would fill that chair.

Asia broke the mood. "There is that skull," she began. Edwin had written of this—how their father had interceded on behalf of a horse thief named Lovett, aiding in his defense, only to lose the case to the hangman. But Lovett with grim gratitude had bequeathed to Booth his skull; now the son who had best known the elder Booth held the memento in his fingers.

John Wilkes took it from him.

"Alas, poor Yorick!" he began, "I knew him, Horatio; a fellow of infinite jest, of most excellent fancy. He hath borne me on his back a thousand times. And now how abhorred in my imagination . . ." All gathered around him and applauded, except Edwin, who sat silent.

When this byplay had ended, the family drew together to dine, and there settled down to cases. For all their father's fame, he had had the squander-lust; accounts were down to a few hundred dollars. Moreover, the farm wasn't producing because, like their father, Asia and Johnny, in trying to manage it, refused to slaughter the stock for sale, and every pig had become a pet.

"There is one thing to do," said Edwin, and then, talking so quickly he could not find time to eat, he outlined his plan for a tour of cities, culminating with a whirlwind booking in New York. That was that.

Johnny looked glum. Well, no matter, said his mother, he had schooling to finish; his time would come. When they had finished listening to Edwin tell of the trials and tribulations of his California and Australian performances, the brothers set about dividing their father's costumes, as was his wish. Here it was a matter of immediate need—what would be best for Edwin's tour—so Johnny was forced to bite his tongue.

Almost at the last came a pair of sparkling spurs bristling with points.

"Ah," said Edwin, "these were mine the first part I played with father, as Tressel, in *Richard III*. Johnny, you take them. For luck."

So John wore them, riding off that night to see his girl. And he would ride with them again, on a night not so happy or so trivial.

The year 1856 had begun well in America. A new railroad headed west across the first thawed ground of spring and inched toward a new bridge over the Mississippi at Rock Island, Illinois. On April 21, to a blare of whistles and a flash of guns, the first train bridged the river into Davenport, Iowa. Soon, said the promoters, steel would span the continent.

In May the spirit of union and progress was shattered: Lawrence, Kansas, was sacked by slavery-party raiders. As John Brown led a retaliatory raid into Missouri Territory, abolitionist fever reached white heat. Secession talk hummed throughout the South.

In March of 1857, the Supreme Court's Dred Scott decision ruled that slaves were noncitizens, without rights. An underground railway pushed northward into Canada as a result, and its success encouraged the abolitionists, deepened southern resentment.

The Washington Monument, begun as a symbol of national unity, stood blunt and futile on the capital skyline, its purpose and its budget snarled in the dispute that would finally become the worst war in our history, killing the most men in proportion to the population.

For Edwin Booth, the 1856–1857 theatrical season was one of qualified success. He played Baltimore, Richmond, Chicago, and Boston, his assurance and his billing improving all the way.

The World's Greatest Actor
The Inheritor of His Father's Genius

In Detroit, his rating seemed to have slipped:

Engagement for One Week Only
of Simple
Edwin Booth

Actually, this mix-up started when Booth complained to the theater manager that he hated elaborate billing, preferring to be described *simply* as "Edwin Booth." One can guess that the manager decided to give

Booth his comeuppance. Perhaps he did. A friend wrote that Booth wore striking suits, cultivated long, curly hair, and smoked huge cigars. "Chain lightning," he said, "couldn't find Edwin in those days."

Booth had acquired fast habits in California. He had drunk a good deal of whiskey, found comfort in women of low reputation. Back East, he declaimed on the virtues of marriage. But, he said, he would never marry an actress.

Then in Richmond he found himself playing Romeo opposite a sweet sixteen-year-old actress, Mary Devlin, a girl under the guardianship of Joe Jefferson, who was to become famous for his characterization of Rip Van Winkle.

"Mother," Booth wrote home, "I have seen and acted with a young woman who has so impressed me that I could almost forget my vow never to marry an actress."

Jefferson had his own opinion of the Booths. However, he admitted in writing, "There is a gentleness and sweetness of manner in him that makes him far more winning than his father."

In the most tender scenes of Shakespeare's play about ill-fated love, the hands of these young actors could scarcely keep from each other.

"Thus from my lips, by thine, my sin is purg'd," said Edwin, kissing her.

"Then have my lips the sin that they have took," she answered.

"Sin from my lips?" he said. "O trespass sweetly urg'd! Give me my sin again." At this she tittered slightly, which was not according to the play.

"You kiss by the book," said Juliet.

"Do I indeed?" said Edwin Booth, *sotto voce.*

Joe Jefferson reacted furiously when he realized that Booth was serious about Mary. Why, all the Booths were lunatics; at least, most of them were.

Mary Devlin may have been tempted to defend her Romeo in Juliet's name:

> 'Tis but thy name that is my enemy;
> Thou art thyself though, not a *Booth.*
> What's a Booth? It is nor hand, nor foot,
> Nor arm, nor face, nor any other part
> Belonging to a man. O, be some other name!

But Edwin realized he could not successfully defend himself against the terrifying reputation of his father. He resorted to humor instead. When Jefferson ordered Mary to return the turquoise bracelet Booth had given her, Edwin bought an identical bracelet, which he gave to Mrs. Jefferson.

A few days later, in a fit of good spirits, the couple took matters in their own hands. Rushing to Jefferson, they fell on their knees, whispering, "Father, your blessing."

Jefferson chuckled. "Bless you, my children," he said. He had been thoroughly softened.

They might have married then if Booth hadn't had to rush off in one direction and Mary in another to keep theatrical engagements. Booth's progress from play to play is recorded in various letters of that time. He realized that he used many of his father's gestures, often awkwardly, and spoke lines as his father had spoken them, without his father's force. When the critics were unkind, as they often were, he took the news philosophically. It was the size of his audiences that bothered him; he could not live well or support his mother and sister Rosalie unless he pulled larger crowds.

Evidence of his poverty survives. A laundry list was used as writing paper. On its reverse, Edwin jotted a note to friend David Anderson. When Anderson had finished reading the message, he turned the paper over, and beside the printed washing list found the following notations: "It's all I own. Don't Weep. Mr. Booth's list of Assets. *Night Shirts:* 0 *Bosoms:* 0 *Drawers:* 1 *Stockings:* 2 *Chemise:* oh *Caps:* hum *Dresses:* he, he *Night Dresses:* law! *Corsets:* Ha ha ha *Capes:* I confess the cape."

Edwin managed to send his letters one jump ahead of Mary Devlin's road stops. He wrote mainly about the theater. His style, he said, was improving, and so was the audience. The critics be damned.

Then in Boston, in April, 1857, the *Transcript* reviewer changed his tune. "Quite a triumph," he wrote. "Young Booth's success was decided. . . . It brought back the most vivid recollections of the fire, the vigor, the strong intellectuality which characterized the acting of his lamented father."

The night after, Booth acted *Richelieu,* a play by Bulwer-Lytton no longer performed today. Julia Ward Howe, who later wrote "The Battle Hymn of the Republic," was in the audience. Nudging her husband, she said, "This is the real thing."

Booth must play New York, now that smaller theaters had welcomed him. An opening in *Richard III* was arranged for the Metropolitan Theatre on lower Broadway in what was then a section of theaters and stores on an open, tree-lined thoroughfare. Here, Edwin rode in a hansom cab; posters lined the way, glued to every fence and shop window:

**Son of the Great Tragedian
Hope of the Living Drama
Richard's Himself Again**

Booth was furious; he had ordered his people to refrain from comparisons. "I'm ruined," he growled.

But at the theater he calmed down. This was his responsibility. These were the people he must please, thronging the streets, spilling from carriages, smiling at one another. How finely dressed they were, and how well-mannered! The intellectuals, too, had appeared to see the son of the great lamented J.B. perform. He slipped down a side street to the stage door, his teeth clenched in determination. This New York opening, now, was his main chance.

Booth's assault on New York show business was ill-timed. Commerce was still in the throes of a depression following the panic of 1857; audiences had been thin. Strange were the attractions concocted to pull them inside theaters.

In May of that year, the bored had their pick of *Fate; or, the Children of Love,* at the Bowery; *Cleopatra; or, the Battle of Actium,* at the National; and a play titled *Neighbor Jackson,* about a runaway slave, at P. T. Barnum's American Museum. The issues of the day entered these plays: "slavery, Mormonism, spiritualism, crime, and the financial crisis."

Into this highly charged, competitive marketplace Booth intruded, a slight, pale youth, with flowing black hair, soft brown eyes full of tenderness, and a manner of mixed shyness and repose. If the public had tired of the rant and roar of Edwin Forrest, they gave little sign of it. Worse, this gentle man faced squarely one of William Shakespeare's most complex characters, Richard III.

One speech of only thirty lines, in which the dream-bound Richard confronts the ghost of Buckingham, is filled with opportunities for subtlety. The king concludes:

And if I die, no soul will pity me:
Nay, wherefore should they, since that I myself
Find in myself no pity to myself?
Methought the souls of all that I had murder'd
Came to my tent; and every one did threat
Tomorrow's vengeance on the head of Richard.

However, one can understand why Edwin Forrest or Junius Brutus Booth chose to deliver the passage with a sledge-hammer force. The bolder style merely simplified the matter of interpretation: catch the meter, and sing it out.

Booth sat for some time in his dressing room, smoking, setting himself to what he must do. He had well chosen, he felt, in deciding to let all hatred and thirst for vengeance seethe beneath the surface. He knew his style ran counter to New York taste.

With a sigh, he extinguished his cigar and turned toward the mirror for the makeup that would transform his features, suggesting the strain of royal office.

As his arms found the sleeves of his costume, Edwin's mind reeled back over the theaters he had played, the leaky roofs, the rats in dressing rooms, the rocking stagecoaches; and he remembered the miles he had traveled—aching, dirty, without food or drink.

In one Midwestern city the temperature had plunged to fifteen below zero. In a heatless theater, a scattered audience in furs and boots stomped to warm their toes, and left the building one by one until only two or three remained for the last act. But Booth had played it for them.

He remembered the catcalls of the California miners. He had played before them in saloons, on a stage of boards set across sawhorses or barrels.

He remembered being snowbound on the road between engagements, when the actors of his troupe had to heave on the harnesses of the horses to help them get through the drifts.

Booth could have quit, let the snow win, but he had promised himself that he would bring the people the great plays as they should be played. So he swept from the boards cheap truncated double and triple Shakespeare bills that were to presage the one-acters of vaudeville. He would bring to the full works of the Bard a greater glory.

Booth's call came. He strode onto the stage of the Metropolitan Theatre. There were faces and faces, hundreds of faces, watching him. Men and women leaning forward. A fog of whispers. The flash of diamonds. Tiny pearl-inlaid opera glasses elevated. The flutter of fans. A ripple of applause at sight of him. Had that been for his father?

He could forget the audience.

> Now is the winter of our discontent
> Made glorious summer by this sun of York.

In moments he could not remember when he had not been king.

> And all the clouds that lour'd upon our house
> In the deep bosom of the ocean buried.
> Now are our brows bound with victorious wreathes;
> Our bruised arms hung up for monuments . . .

"An unqualified triumph," said the *Herald*. Sleepless and tense, Booth read the words in the early morning. He had captivated the crowd from the moment of his first appearance, they said. His voice, they went on to say, was thrillingly musical. His acting was remarkable for its freedom and boldness.

But farther down, he noted qualifications: that his style suggested his father at every turn of phrase, and that he lacked the "scoffing, sardonic, humorous mockery" suitable to the role.

In later years he would admit that these early performances were imitations of his father. Now he set out to transform himself, to peel off, layer by layer, the influence of those years on the road with J.B.

Booth needed to restudy Romeo. When he appeared in Boston in March, 1858, in that role, he gave a fairly convincing performance. "The two true lovers were at their best," wrote Julia Ward Howe, "ideally young, beautiful and identified with their parts."

Booth, of course, had played again opposite Mary Devlin.

Yet he held back from marriage, as much from devotion to his work as out of caution. Evenings, on a large bear rug before the fire, Edwin read and reread his speeches to Mary's cue lines.

When it came to romance, John Wilkes Booth was another story. He, too, was touring, leaving behind a trail of broken hearts, but also skeptical critics and infuriated abolitionists.

One actress attacked him with a knife, almost disfiguring his hand-

Edwin and John Wilkes Booth, brothers who took opposite roles onstage and in politics
Lithograph by A. Hoen & Co.
Photograph, C. Fredricks & Co., New York

some face. Another, rejected, attempted suicide by swallowing chloroform.

Wherever he acted, North or South, Johnny spoke for the southern cause. In one northern city, an angered cast threatened to close the show if he did not stop propagandizing.

His temper became a matter of record among his associates. In stage duels he fought with grim reality. His opponents often had to bruise or nick him with their blades to keep the contest center stage.

Once he threw himself down on the stage so hard that he cut himself with his own dagger. Another time, in a fit of pique, he threw a scenery wedge at the prompter, narrowly missing his head.

Edwin seemed blind to John's faults. When their paths crossed, they performed together: October, 1857, Edwin's Hamlet with John Wilkes's Horatio.

At the end of this drama, with the death of Hamlet, Horatio spoke prophetically in the person of the younger Booth:

> Let me speak to the yet unknown world
> How these things came about. So shall you hear
> Of carnal, bloody, and unnatural acts,
> Of accidental judgments, casual slaughters;
> Of deaths put on by cunning and forc'd cause,
> And, in this upshot, purposes mistook
> Fallen on the inventors' heads; all this can I
> Truly deliver.

The nation drifted apart, North from South, and as it did, so did the brothers. In the North, Edwin was praised; generally, John was not. He acted more and more in the South—Richmond, Charleston, or Baltimore. Often he billed himself in a way that would dissociate him from his brothers and father:

J. Wilkes Booth
I Am Myself Alone

When Edwin finally married Mary Devlin, the family was further split by Asia, who accused Mary of getting Edwin Booth drunk in order to make him propose. All she wanted, said Asia, was the family name.

The wedding took place quietly on July 7, 1860. The following November, Abraham Lincoln was elected President.

The events of the next five years form an incredible panorama. We see John Wilkes Booth in Albany, acting, sounding out against Lincoln, and being put down. We see him in the crowd as the President-elect passes through the city. Scorn is on his face.

We see Edwin in London performing, and going to his wife's side after the birth of their daughter, Edwina. We see him setting sail for America, now in the midst of a worsening war, in his pocket the letters of his mother urging the family to remain together. Johnny has grown more radical. Joseph, she writes, has actually served as a doctor during the attack on Fort Sumter.

In the war days, we see John traveling north and south, passing through the lines on his actor's credentials in order to disguise his role as a smuggler of medical supplies.

John seemed driven to prove himself. John Ellsler, manager of the Cleveland Theatre and a booster of Edwin Forrest, liked John's flamboyant style. "He has more of the old man's power in one performance than Edwin can show in a year," he said. "He has the fire, the dash, the touch of strangeness." With some others, he considered Edwin tame, disliking the intellectual approach that he took to tragic character. This faction failed to realize that in America, with the decline of Forrest and the rejection of his type of bombastic style, there had begun a return to Shakespeare's original text and a deeper understanding of the characters.

Given this direction, the theater might work through to the kind of characterization where a king, in quiet soliloquy, became mere man. Common men, much later, would become the subjects of great plays in the American theater.

But the new age, an age of naturalism foreshadowed by Edwin Booth in his rendition of Shakespeare, was far off. So John Wilkes could be sure of a following, particularly in the South, and even Edwin had to be careful that his scenes of violence and wrath were violent or wrathful enough to please the gallery.

Despite the controversy over style, we see Edwin rising in his profession, completely absorbed in its challenge, with Mary supporting him in every way.

Edwin's mastery increased. A certain relaxation set in. New York and Boston society accepted Mr. and Mrs. Booth. Though he remained shy and withdrawn at parties, perpetuating the myth that he *was* the gloomy Dane, Hamlet, he shattered that myth at times by revelry with his wife among close friends. There he played the delightful host, witty and engaging, friend of artists, writers, musicians, famous for his ease, and for his habit of making atrocious puns.

Sometimes he drank a little too much. Would he go to the bottle as his father had? Critic Adam Badeau and actor William Winter, his closest friends, feared for him.

Booth controlled himself, despite the pressure of his work, because of his marriage. One incident shows how close he and Mary were.

One night while his wife sat in her box absorbed in *Hamlet,* Booth, temporarily offstage, appeared suddenly behind her.

"Lady, shall I lie in your lap?" She started. She whispered, but no louder: "No, my lord."

"I mean, my head upon your lap?" Now he almost shouted as, high above the pit, they acted this bit from *Hamlet,* Act III, Scene 2.

"You are merry, my lord," she said. "Shhh. Not so loud. They'll hear you."

"What should a man do but be merry?" he carried on. "For, look you, how cheerfully my mother looks, and my father died within two hours."

Now faces had turned upward, and there were titters. As quickly as he had come, with a kiss, he left her.

Their love was profound, their communion deep. When he began a long engagement in Boston, she went with him, and so did little Edwina.

During the Boston run, Mary Booth became weak, thin, pale. Edwin took her to Dr. Erasmus Miller, a noted Dorchester expert in tubercular cases. Miller assured them that although his diagnosis was as they had feared, it was a light case, and with rest and time, nothing serious would come of it.

Mary stayed in Dorchester with a nurse and Edwina, to be in Dr. Miller's care. "He has inspired me with a great deal of faith," she wrote. "All agree that he is wonderful."

Edwin went on to New York, where he worked and worried. He planned outings for spring when Mary would be well.

In the dead of winter, she wrote, "I've laid all my plans for a home next winter in New York. . . . I do nothing all day but lay out bright visions of the future; it pleases me beyond all things to dream thus—but experience has taught me that it is all folly. We are masters of our destiny only to a very small extent."

John Wilkes Booth seemed to be riding high. Extolled in the South, he now invaded the North, and in January, 1863, appeared in Boston as the evil Pescara in *The Apostate.* Bundling Mary up carefully, Edwin Booth managed to get her to see the performance. "A bloody villain of the deepest red," said Edwin. "He is full of the true grit. I am delighted with him."

Edwin returned to New York to work, but news came that Mary had weakened. He could not leave his play. Whiskey numbed his anxiety.

"Seldom have we seen Shakespeare so murdered as at the Winter

Garden during the past two weeks," said the New York *Herald*. "It would have been better to disappoint the public by closing the theater than to place Mr. Booth upon the stage when he was really unfit to act."

One night, John Wilkes himself traveled from Mary's side to tell Edwin how she had foolishly gone to Boston to see a friend, how the horsecar had been bogged down in heavy snow, and while waiting for it, Mary had taken a bad chill.

Telegrams came in due course from Dorchester. They lay, three of them, unopened on Booth's dressing-room table. He had not, in his stupor, the strength or courage to open them. That evening, February 20, he played *Richard III* in a trance.

But friends had been telegraphed too, and they broke through to Edwin, dosed him with coffee, and put him on a train.

When he arrived at Dorchester, he said to those who met him, "Don't tell me, I know."

He spent the entire night with her dead body.

Months later, he wrote, "My child should be a solace to me, but *she,* alas! was my child, my baby-wife. . . . Oh, Dick, only to think I've locked her up in a box and have the key of it; it doesn't seem as though she were in a coffin, does it?"

It has been said that in the two-year interval between Mary's death and the assassination of Lincoln, Edwin Booth laid the foundation of his greatness, that he made of his profession a monument to his lost wife.

His grief brought understanding. Hard maturing changed what had been a hollow reading of many of Shakespeare's most difficult passages. At thirty-two Edwin walked onstage an older man.

It was in this interval that he gave a series of performances of *Hamlet* in New York that lasted one hundred days. It was as *the* Booth that he commanded his brothers to appear with him in *Julius Caesar* for the benefit of the Shakespeare statue to be placed in Central Park. John Wilkes even had to shave off his moustache.

Edwin became so well known that even among the crowds and in the dim lighting of a railroad station he was easily recognized.

Late in the winter of 1865, in one of those incredible ironies of life, Edwin saved a stranger from falling between cars as they moved in the thronged Jersey City railway terminal.

"That was a narrow escape, Mr. Booth," said the young stranger.

Later, Booth learned that he had saved the life of Robert Lincoln, son of the President.

John Wilkes Booth's mood had soared with the fortunes of his southern friends in arms. Gen. Robert E. Lee seemed invincible. President Lincoln had to relieve general after general of the Union command. When much seemed lost, Ulysses S. Grant appeared on the horizon. By advancing through Tennessee, the Union forces led by General Grant laid Vicksburg, Mississippi, under siege. The Confederacy, anticipating Vicksburg's fall and the elimination of Tennessee from the war, approved Lee's plan for a daring march northward into Union territory.

Having a foothold in Pennsylvania, Lee sent Ewell toward York. John Wilkes Booth laughed as he read the dispatches in the newspapers. He guffawed as if at a good joke when he learned that the city had fallen to Ewell and that the people were laid under contribution and forced to "donate" to the Rebel cause 1,000 hats, 1,200 pairs of shoes, 1,000 socks, and three days' rations.

By June 29, with seventy-five thousand on Pennsylvania soil, Lee swung toward Harrisburg, the state capital, then turned his main army toward Gettysburg to avoid General Meade.

The battle of Gettysburg began July 1 and ended July 3, 1863, culminating in Pickett's charge against the Union fortifications. Frank Haskell of the Second Corps, against which the charge was directed, described the scene:

> Every eye could see the enemy's legions, an overwhelming resistless tide of an ocean of armed men sweeping upon us . . . the arms of eighteen thousand men, barrel and bayonet, gleam in the sun, a sloping forest of flashing steel. Right on they move, as with one soul, in perfect order, without impediment of ditch or wall or stream, over ridge and slope, through orchard and meadow and cornfield, magnificent, grim, irresistible.

Such newspaper accounts John Wilkes Booth read with terrible fear— how the Union artillery had waited in readiness and "opened fire upon the advancing column at 700 yards and continued until it came to close quarters."

A barrage of cannister shot. Outright slaughter. But the remnant pressed forward. General Armistead rushed forward to plant the Confederate colors on the Union wall, and fighting over the wall became hand to hand. But the Union line held. "All this has been my fault," Robert E. Lee said. "It is I that have lost this fight." The war tide had turned.

Now John Wilkes's career took a peculiar twist. In 1859, at Titusville, in Pennsylvania, oil had been discovered. During the war, the oil rush gained momentum, and in September, 1864, John Wilkes Booth made his appearance in Franklin, hub of this activity.

With Booth came John Ellsler, Cleveland theater owner, and one Joseph H. Simonds. Settled at a hotel, they frequented shops, real estate offices, and saloons, like other oil hounds gathering rumor.

Booth was immediately recognized by people who had seen him onstage. Was he here to perform? No, he said confidentially, he must invest wisely to assure some income separate from the stage. A sharp move, they nodded. Any sensible financier could see that.

Venango County stirred with news of the famous actor, for stage actors then were regarded as motion picture stars are now. Where would the tragedian put his money?

At depths of only a few hundred feet, the brown gold might be struck, bringing the landowner thousands in sudden profits. Distilled, the crude petroleum produced a lighting oil almost as good as whale oil, and considerably cheaper. Booth's choice was the farm of Thomas and Wilhelmina Mears. These fortunate people pocketed his gold and held their ears. Soon the drill was pounding, hitched to a whomping steam engine.

Foot by foot the steel drove down.

"I'll call her the Wilhelmina," Booth decided. "No. *Better*. The Dramatic Oil Company."

Not long after, oil began to flow lazily to the surface. Booth peered into the syrupy puddle; then he spat. Why wouldn't the stuff come faster? He had expected success, but this was no gusher. Yet oil was oil. They drilled deeper. Booth, in gentleman's clothes, his shirt sleeves rolled to the elbow, labored with the men. None of his oaths and speeches would make the oil ooze faster.

Aboard a ferry one day, Booth was caught up in a fistfight over an antisouthern remark.

Back at the well, nothing improved.

"Why not dynamite her, Mr. Booth?" the driller asked.

"What for?"

"To open the rock, improve the flow."

"Good, good," said John Wilkes. "We'll get her going now."

The explosion, muffled in the earth, was hardly cataclysmic. Neither was the result. Not one drop of oil flowed afterward, and the well had to be abandoned.

John was furious over this failure—he had counted on the money to finance his plot to kidnap Lincoln and the Secretary of State. Joseph Simonds, his agent in Franklin, tried to straighten him out:

"Your strange note of the 16th rec'd. I hardly know what to make of you this winter—so different from your usual self. Have you lost all your ambition or what is the matter? Don't get offended with me John but I cannot but think you are wasting your time spending the entire season in Washington doing nothing where it must be expensive to live and all for no other purpose beyond pleasure."

To himself, however, John's purpose was ample.

On the fourth of June, 1864, at the McHenry House, a hotel in northwestern Pennsylvania, in Meadville, a guest signed the register, "John Wilkes Booth."

Sometime after, it was discovered that he had scratched the following message on the windowpane of his room, using his diamond ring as a cutter:

"Abe Lincoln departed this life August 13th, 1864, by the effects of poison." This piece of glass and the signature were given to the government in 1879.

Evidence shows that John had plotted the death of the President for at least a year.

John lived in a room in the National Hotel in Washington. At the boardinghouse of Mrs. Mary Surratt on H Street, he conspired with young Michael O'Laughlin and Sam Arnold, with whom he had gone to school, and dull-witted David Herold, and carriage-maker George A. Atzerodt, and Lewis Paine, a Confederate deserter.

Two plans for kidnapping fell through.

By April, 1865, Richmond was lost. John faced toward that city crying hysterically, "Virginia, Virginia!" Later his sister, Asia, wrote, "If Wilkes Booth was mad, his mind lost its balance between the fall of Richmond and the terrific end."

Visiting Asia, he raged against Lincoln, calling him a dictator. In Boston, he visited Edwin. They wrangled over the war. "Good-by, Ted," he said. "You and I could never agree about that." They would not meet again.

Their mother had gone to live with Edwin. She wrote John a letter that may have been her last.

"I never yet doubted your love and devotion to me—in fact I always gave you praise for being the fondest of all my boys, but since you leave me to grief I must doubt it. I am no Roman mother. I love my dear ones before country or anything else. Heaven guard you, is my constant prayer."

In March, John visited in the room of Charley Warwick, an actor who boarded across the street from Ford's Theatre. There he collapsed late at night in a stupor from drinking.

"Who would think," Warwick wrote, "to look on that handsome face, so calm and peaceful in repose, that beneath it slumbered a volcano? Who could raise the curtain of the near future and peer upon the picture of the dying President on that very bed?"

On April 11, John Wilkes Booth stood in a crowd on the White House lawn listening to Lincoln speak on giving the ballot to the Negro. "Nigger citizenship!" he said to his friend Herold. "Now, by God, I'll put him through!"

It was spring of 1865 on the Potomac. The terrible war had ended. Now the President moved freely among society. On the evening of April 14 he and Mrs. Lincoln and two guests went to Ford's Theatre to see a play. As they took their seats in a flag-draped box, they were given an ovation. The President sat near the back of the box in his rocking chair.

In the saloon next to Ford's Theatre, Booth drank brandy.

"You'll never be the actor your father was!" an actor friend teased him.

"When I leave the stage, I'll be the most famous man in America," said Booth. He had the pistol in his pocket then.

John Wilkes Booth easily entered the theater ticketless, for he had acted there many times and knew the doorman. Lincoln's guard had gone to the gallery to watch the play. Booth opened the door to the President's box. He fired a single shot. The President's head dropped forward on his chest as though he were asleep.

The play was *Our American Cousin,* a popular comedy. Starring was

Laura Keene, who had played opposite Edwin in California. Also in the cast was George Spear, who in California had broken the news to Edwin of his father's death.

Moments before the shot, the following lines were spoken:

> MRS. MOUNTCHESSINGTON: I am aware, Mr. Trenchard, that you are not used to the manner of good society, and that alone will excuse the impertinence of which you have been guilty.
>
>   *(Exit. Trenchard, left alone, soliloquizes.)*
>
> TRENCHARD: Don't know the manners of good society, eh? Well, I guess I know enough to turn you inside out, old gal—you sockdologizing old mantrap.

At this moment, a thin wisp of smoke issued from Lincoln's box, which was curtained from the audience. Within the box, two figures grappled—Booth and a Major Rathbone. Slashing with a dagger, Booth broke free, and then hurled himself into the air toward the stage. As he did so, one of his spurs caught in the Union flag draping the box, so that he landed awkwardly, breaking one ankle.

The spurs he wore were the pair Edwin had worn in his first stage appearance.

In that dismal night their tines pricked the hide of a fleeing horse as John Wilkes Booth clattered across the cobbles of the capital.

6
Edwin Booth, Star

THE NEWS PASSED with feverish speed among the acting community: Edwin Booth, brother of Lincoln's murderer, would return to the stage. It had been set for January 3, 1866. An antiactor faction in New York rallied its forces when it learned that Booth had decided to face the public at the Winter Garden.

The New York *Herald,* a sanctum of prudery, seemed to enjoy its opportunity: "Is the Assassination of Caesar to be Performed? Will Booth appear as the assassin of Caesar? That would be, perhaps, the most suitable character."

Edwin Booth wondered, as he read these notices, whether his return to the stage was well advised. There were stories of mob activity, of extra details of police.

Yet he and his family so desperately needed money that he must take the risk.

Friends who had urged before, urged again, "Give it up, Edwin." He must no longer endanger his immortal soul in the court of the devil, for that was what the playhouse was. Repent while time remained. Take up the ministry. What better use for his voice and talent than speaking the word of God from the pulpit?

The night of January 3 drew near. He had chosen *Hamlet,* his most sympathetic role, and would appear first sitting in the king's court, instead of making a stage entrance, in order that the audience remain calm.

Edwin could understand those who argued against the stage. Devoted to the classics, he saw in the theaters of his time vice and corruption.

At Niblo's that season *The Black Crook* ran for four hundred and seventy-four performances. The show boasted girls who, for the first time in a leading house, wore tights—without skirts.

In that season of forty-nine plays, *It Is Never Too Late to Mend* was the big hit. Others were *Still Waters Run Deep, Miriam's Crime, Deaf as a Post, Rural Felicity,* and *High Life Below the Stairs.*

Still the *Herald* raved on against Booth: "Shame upon such indecent and reckless disregard of propriety and the sentiments of the American people! Can the sinking fortunes of this foreign manager be sustained in no other way than by such an indecent violation of propriety? The blood of our martyred President is not yet dry in the memory of the people, and the very name of the assassin is appalling to the public mind; still a Booth is advertised to appear before a New York audience!"

Hamlet readied himself within his room. He buckled on his sword. With some irony he contemplated the situation—how he, the brother of the villain who slew Lincoln, must appear and speak as Hamlet to the ghost of Hamlet's father:

"Revenge his foul and most unnatural murder," the ghost would say.
"Murder!" Hamlet would say.

> Murder most foul, as in the best it is;
> But this most foul, strange, and unnatural.

Booth knew how inflammatory this could seem to an audience come to hate him, as though this were the ghost of Lincoln himself. Then, he, Hamlet, would say,

> Haste me to know't, that I, with wings as swift
> As meditation or the thoughts of love,
> May sweep to my revenge.

But how could this audience understand how impossible it had been for him to join the nation's lust for revenge? He still kept a picture of the assassin; he had been his brother. Ought he to have appeared at the execution of the plotters? Should he have stood up at the trial, and taken *there* a bow, a bow of apology? Now he could hear the audience, from backstage, hear the rumble of what must be their discontent.

He hoped they had read and could remember the public statement he had made—if only more newspapers had published it at that awful time!

Booth's proclamation was regarded by intelligent observers as a most unusual document. As a crosslight into personal crisis, it was without parallel. As Booth trembled, waiting to meet an audience calm during the

The handsome actor Edwin Booth, and his dramatic signature on the next page, are from an engraving by H. B. Hall, Jr., New York.

appearance of minor characters in the first scene, its wording came to him line by line, as though he must set himself now in the tone of that apology:

To the People of the United States: My Fellow Citizens

When a nation is overwhelmed with sorrow by a great public calamity, the mention of private grief would under ordinary circumstances be an intrusion, but under those by which I am surrounded, I feel sure that a word from me will not be so regarded by you.

It has pleased God to lay at the door of my afflicted family the life blood of our deservedly popular President. Crushed to very earth by this dreadful event, I am yet but too sensible that other mourners are in the land. To them, to you one and all, go forth our deep, unutterable sympathy; our abhorrence and detestation of this most foul and atrocious crime.

For my mother and sister, my two remaining brothers and my poor self, there is nothing to be said except that we are thus placed without any agency of our own. For our loyalty as dutiful, though humble, citizens as well as for our consistent and, as we had some reason to believe, successful efforts to elevate our name personally and professionally, we appeal to the record of the past. For our present position we are not responsible. For the future—alas! I shall struggle on in my retirement bearing a heavy heart, an oppressed memory and a wounded name— dreadful burdens—to my too welcome grave.

Edwin Booth

Booth's first thought had been for his loved ones. On May 6, 1865, ten days after John Wilkes had been trapped in a barn in Virginia, driven out by fire, and shot, Edwin wrote a friend:

I've just received your letter. I have been in one sense unable to write, but you know, of course, what my condition is, and need no excuses.

I have been, by the advice of my friends, "cooped up" since I arrived here [Boston], going out only occasionally in the evening. My health is good, but I suffer from the want of fresh air and exercise.

Poor mother is in Philadelphia, about crushed by her sorrows, and my sister, Mrs. Clarke, is ill and without the least knowledge of her husband, who was taken from her several days ago, with Junius. [Edwin was not arrested, though his trunks were searched.]

My position is such a delicate one that I am obliged to use the utmost caution. Hosts of friends are stanch and true to me. . . . I feel safe. What I am in Phila. and elsewhere I know not. . . . My baby [Edwina] . . . is there. Now that the greatest excitement is over, and a lull is in the storm, I feel the need of that dear angel; but during the heat of it I was glad she was not here.

When Junius and Mr. Clarke are at liberty, mother will come here and bring Edwina to me.

I wish I could see with others' eyes; all my friends assure me that my name shall be free and that in a little while I may be where I was and what I was; but, alas! it looks dark to me.

Now as Booth prepared to walk again upon a stage, he could hear police arguing as latecomers tried to wedge their way into the jammed house. What a happier occasion it had been, and what a great crowd, in 1864, when he and John and Junius had appeared in this same theater in *Julius Caesar,* and he had bowed toward the box where his mother sat!

When Mrs. Booth received the news of Lincoln's death, she thought only as a mother. "O God, if this be true," she said, "let him [John] shoot himself. Let him not live to be hanged."

Minutes later the postman brought a letter written by John the day before:

I only drop you these few lines to let you know I am well. . . . With best love to you all I am your affectionate son ever.

This was his normal side. Actors who had known and liked him were not so quick to cast him off. One wrote, "He was so young, so bright, so gay. . . . Many a painted cheek showed runnels made by bitter tears." How then must his mother have felt?

Booth wrote to another friend:

It is a great blessing that I have had so much occupation all this while, else I should have gone mad, I fear. My poor mother feels her woe greater than she shows, and I fear all her life is crushed by this last terrible one. . . . I have no idea when, if ever, I shall act again.

And in another letter:

Mother is very much broken, I think, poor soul! . . . She seems to have still a lingering hope in her heart that all this will prove to be a dream.

And finally, in December, 1865, two weeks before his return to the stage:

> Let it pass; life is a great big spelling-book, and on every page we turn the words grow harder to understand the meaning of. But there *is* a meaning, and when the last leaf flops over, we'll know the whole lesson by heart.
>
> You have also, doubtless, heard that I will soon appear on the stage. Sincerely, were it not for means, I would not do so . . . but I have huge debts to pay . . . a love for the grand and beautiful in art . . . to gratify.

So he had decided.

Now he walked toward the stage. Horatio and the others came hurrying out past him, with a penetrating look, or a touch upon the arm. All the business of the set went on while he, oblivious, looked out from the wings toward the place where he must place himself again, subject to approval.

Weighted, the early scenery flew, and papier-mâché stones were kicked about. The trappings of court and ornate chairs were slid into place. He with other actors found their spots. Before them the curtain hung dark and reassuring; they all knew the significance of this moment.

The audience did not, for a time, differentiate between Polonius and Laertes. Then he moved and spoke aside, directly to the audience, after the King said:

"But now, my cousin Hamlet, and my son—"

"A little more than kin, and less than kind," said Hamlet quietly.

Now they knew him.

As a man the people rose to cheer.

There were shouts and cries of delight. Those who stood silent may have been supposed to come to hiss; they did not.

As at last the din subsided, someone gave a shout:

"Three groans for the New York *Herald*!" Three liberal boos vibrated the hall, followed by a swell of laughter.

Silence.

Booth stood and gravely bowed. His eyes filled with tears at this acceptance.

This was not enough—no praise would be enough, nor were the critics unanimous in praising his acting now—to lift the weight from Edwin's shoulders. In company, he was quiet. He cared for his mother. He paid bills, even to the point of reimbursing the Virginia farmer whose barn had been burned to drive out his brother.

When the Winter Garden caught fire the morning after a performance, Booth walked calmly behind the engines and crowds as though enjoying the spectacle. "Not a wig left," he said easily.

In utter objectivity, in the same deadly quiet, he had set out to wrest John Wilkes's body from the government. He wrote to Ulysses S. Grant, who had become Secretary of War:

> Sir—I now appeal to you—on behalf of my heart-broken mother— that she may receive the remains of her son. You, Sir, can understand what a consolation it would be to an aged parent to have the privilege of visiting the grave of her child.

Though Grant had promised to help Booth in any way, he did not answer this letter. Booth wrote again and again. President Andrew Johnson finally acquiesced.

There was one sure explanation for Booth's calm, resolve, and de termination. He had found another Juliet. Mary McVicker was the fiery stepdaughter of James McVicker, manager of a Chicago theater where Booth had played years before and she, a ragtag child, had pulled him into silly games.

As an actress, she had crossed his path several times; now his tragic life drew her close. With a fine, robust sense of humor this new Mary drew him out of himself.

Caught in a wave of optimism, Booth aligned backers for the construction of a new theater, The Booth, at Twenty-third Street and Sixth Avenue. Its completion created a monstrous debt. He envisioned a temple to Shakespeare, and that is what he built.

The foyer was sheathed in marble. Three towers rose above, flying banners. Inside all was luxury: a tremendous fan run by steam circulated air among the audience; hydraulic engines drove the backdrops up through slots in the stage, so that no sets had to be "flown."

The critics were unkind. Booth and Mary opened in *Romeo and Juliet,* and readers were reminded that Romeo was not Edwin's strongest role.

"Mr. Booth merely drifts through excellent stage business and wonderfully maneuvered machinery with hackneyed motions, caught or conveyed, without any regard to the character as a whole," wrote one critic, who did not have a kind word for Mary, either: "Miss Mary McVicker, for whom Mr. Booth thus gallantly sacrificed himself, we are pained to say, is in no way worthy of the sacrifice. She is no delicate geranium."

The house made money, however, though not enough to meet its huge expenses. Booth remained optimistic, seeming to have turned his back on the past, and when John Wilkes's body was at last released to the family, he played as little part as possible.

A telegram arrived in February, 1869: "Successful and in our possession." Edwin folded it for filing and on it wrote simply: "John's Body."

On June 7 of that year, Edwin and Mary McVicker were married.

On June 26, Edwin, his mother, and brother and sisters gathered at Greenmount Cemetery, Baltimore, to inter John's remains. Several actors, true to their profession, carried the coffin.

An Episcopal minister came in from New York to speak over the grave. He had not thought to ask who was to be buried, and when he found out, it was too late.

He was expelled by his congregation.

The past had been buried and if for Edwin no new grief had come, he might have found, with the healing of old wounds, some joy in life.

Mary McVicker Booth had retired from the stage; no fear now that her ever-available Juliet would press him into an uncomfortable Romeo. He could play instead Iago, an evil presence releasing from him into the air above his spellbound audiences some of that poison with which fate had injected him.

So he was lost in his grand and beautiful art.

His marriage was happy. And Mary announced one evening that she was going to have a baby.

But the confinement of her pregnancy, the clumsy weight of the baby within her, tormented this woman who was so used to gaiety, freedom.

Worse, the fetus lay within her four weeks beyond normal term, prodding and kicking happily enough, as though content to remain indefinitely. Experts had come and gone, with official black bags and stethoscopes. They shook their heads. Nature would decide.

Mary's labor began.

Edwin was jubilant. Then as the rhythmic contractions speeded and strengthened, hour after hour passed without passage of the child into the hands of the waiting midwife.

As he rebuilt his career after the assassination, Edwin Booth also built a new theater, The Booth, in New York, "a temple to Shakespeare." Engraving from photo by Rockwood, *Harper's Weekly*, January 9, 1869

The physician must use instruments, forceps with which to grasp and retrieve this large baby. Mary was given chloroform. More time passed.

Edwin heard squalling.

But before he could feel reassured the doctor was with him, telling of damage to this boy. Yes, a boy, but hurt by the instruments.

"How badly?"

"Quite badly."

Hours later the child died.

Mary did not respond. For a long while her life hung in the balance. When her strength had returned, she realized that the baby was gone and became hysterical. From then on nervousness and hysteria controlled her behavior, behavior with which she dominated Edwin and her step-daughter, Edwina.

For himself, Edwin Booth was again lost in work and in his love for Edwina, in whom he saw everything he had worshiped in Mary Devlin, whom she resembled.

Booth realized that he had entered a long last chapter of life, one to be marked by a struggle to hold his audiences, to perfect his roles, to meet the demands of his profession—constant travel, duels, dramatic leaps—in a declining body.

Booth met his responsibilities with a humor rare and wry. Few men have labored under such a weight of responsibility and awful memory. Few have so sharpened wit as a weapon against despair.

Mired in debt, the Booth Theatre badly needed elegant stars who could draw the crowd. Creditors argued for the installment of popular melodrama. Booth fought for the classics, eventually persuading the redoubtable Charlotte Cushman to end a ten years' retirement.

In letter after letter she dickered coyly, referring to the advice of doctors on rare illnesses and closing with requests for fantastically high fees. Written in a dainty hand, on scented violet stationery, the notes seemed to come from a petite girl. Actually, Cushman was statuesque, an Amazon.

She consented at last. She would appear as Lady Macbeth, treacherous wife of the assassin, Macbeth, played by Booth. In Act I, Macbeth's courage falters.

"If we should *fail?*" said Booth timidly.

"We *fail!*" hissed Cushman. "But screw your courage to the sticking place. . . . What cannot you and I perform upon the unguarded Duncan? what not put upon his spongy officers, who shall bear the guilt of our great quell?"

Cushman seemed to tower over him.

After the play, Booth's wit convulsed his friends: "I was half tempted to turn to her and say, 'Why don't *you* kill him—you're *bigger* than I am.'"

Booth came to use his humor for defense against the worst possible setbacks. Acting in Chicago in the theater of his father-in-law, Booth presented a flawless *Richard II* to an audience ecstatic except for one man.

The morose young king, imprisoned, is speaking a soft soliloquy:

"And here is not a creature but myself—"

A shot rang out, fired from the balcony. It missed Booth by inches. Another shot missed as he stood up.

Booth walked calmly to the footlights, pointed at his assailant and shouted, "Arrest that man!" He was seized while aiming for the kill.

Mark Gray was a lunatic. He told police he was defending his sister's honor. Once the papers had played that to the skies, he changed his story: he was Booth's illegitimate son. Finally, he explained his attack in no uncertain terms. In an earlier performance, Booth had read the line, "Mark where she stands." He had slurred the name *Mark*. That was enough; he must die.

Booth pried one of the bullets out of a backdrop, had it mounted in a gold setting with the inscription: "From Mark Gray to Edwin Booth." He wore it as a watch fob everywhere he went.

How Booth managed to maintain his sense of fun, no one can guess. He was an elaborate and painful punner, and a welcome guest in the company of artists, architects, and writers, who kept him diverted, and he them, during the last years of Mary McVicker's life, when in paranoid hallucinations she saw Edwin as her mortal enemy. Time and again she drove him from the apartment they shared above the Booth Theatre when he was playing in New York.

When debt forced disposal of the Booth Theatre, Edwin drifted, homeless. His most precious time he spent with his daughter, Edwina, who had married and had two small children.

Sometimes on tour she had traveled with him, though not when he played in London, Paris, or Germany. Once she traveled in the Midwest with the troupe in a private Pullman train.

Of Booth's humor and his tenderness toward Edwina, his letters to his daughter bear testimony. Leafing through them, one can chart the latter years of Booth's life.

Before Edwina became twelve, he wrote her:

> When I was learning to act tragedy, I had frequently to perform comic parts, in order to acquire a certain ease of manner that my serious parts might not appear too stilted; so you must endeavor in your letters, in your conversation, and in your general deportment, to be easy and natural, graceful and dignified. But remember that dignity does not consist of over-becoming pride and haughtiness; self-respect, politeness and gentleness in all things and to all persons will give you sufficient dignity. Well, I declare, I've dropped into a sermon, after all, haven't I?
>
> > Love and kisses from Y'r grim old father.

Booth wrote to her from New York regarding his acting, in 1875:

> My forty-second birthday (yesterday) was passed (day and evening) in the theatre, with Richelieu and Shylock, two weary old boys. I hoped to have photos taken in *Richard II,* the costumes are so beautiful, and your Pop appears as a blond in that character; I will give it in Philadelphia, so that you shall have a chance to behold my flaxen curls. You must read that portion of English history so as to be a little familiar with the tragedy. My friends are enthusiastic over my performance of it. My engagement is very fine, and could be extended here, did I not wish to be with you as soon as possible.

A particularly moving letter was written from Richmond, Virginia, January, 1876:

> 'T was in this city, darling, just twenty years ago, that I first met your angel mother, who now watches over and prays for us in heaven. Twenty years make a large gap in one's lifetime, yet they slip away very quickly, and when gone we wonder how little we have accomplished. . . . My last visit here was seventeen years ago (before you knew me), and the people are greatly excited over my coming. Your grandfather Booth was much beloved here, and made his first appearance before an American audience in this city. You see, I have cause to feel much interest in Richmond.

His letters often contained advice:

> Thoughtfulness is a virtue . . . an anxious care for the feelings of

others is productive of much happiness to ourselves. . . . Tom Hood says:

> There's much harm wrought
> By want of thought
> As there is by want of heart,

or something to this effect; the words may be differently set. . . . "Love thyself last," Shakespeare says, and what he says is about as full of solid sense as any advice which man can give.

The letters continue in this vein until the death of Edwin's mother, the gentle, determined Mary Anne Holmes who lived a most unusual life.

New York, October 22, 1885

Darling:

Poor Grandma passed away at three this morning. I did not arrive till seven. . . . The doctor, yesterday, did not think it necessary to send for me then. She fell into a stupor about 7:30 last night, and died so at three. . . . Although this is a sad blow to me, I have been prepared a long time for it, and the knowledge of her release from suffering is a comfort. 'T is for poor Rose [his maiden sister] I feel most anxious. She has just sighed, barely loud enough for me to hear, "I wish I was gone, too." Poor, poor soul! I must now arrange something for her. I am waiting for the doctor and the embalmers; I can't endure the idea of placing the body on ice.

I managed to sleep pretty well last night, and was not at all fatigued. You must not be anxious for me in the least. I am well, and accept this sorrow with calmness. 'T is my nature to be always expecting death, and when he comes, he does not much surprise me. Besides, I have always regarded the "change" as a blessing rather than a loss. God bless you, darling!

Papa

The years flew by. Hasty notes and long ones marked their passing:

The audience was delighted with everything. . . . Hamlet tomorrow, Iago next. This is the same room I had last year. . . . I hope, dear, that you and the babies continue well, and that you will enjoy many, many happy years in your charming little home. Love to you all.

Edwin Booth as Richelieu. Gravure by Gebbie & Husson Co., Ltd.

From Minneapolis, September, 1887:

> Last night my engagement closed with a crowded house; it has been an extraordinary week of great success. . . . We do not leave until 8 A.M. tomorrow for Duluth. The "Crickets" [critics] here persistently "go for" my antiquity, while praising me otherwise. . . . Poor Hammy [Hamlet] must soon be laid away in camphor in a dark corner cupboard.
>
> I have a cold that checks my breathing, and I sit with my mouth agape like a blooming idiot.

Booth had reached fifty-four. Tall and spare, but not strong, he suffered colds. A fall from a horse had broken his left arm, which, badly set, had to be rebroken and set again. This came out shorter than the right, and could not be raised fully. He writes:

> We hope to get a run of Caesar and of Othello; Brutus and Iago being quiet parts. . . . By doing the fifth act of *The Merchant of Venice* with some new scenes . . . we may get several nights and matinees out of Shylock also, the three easiest of my characters. . . . This city seems to grow more beautiful. . . . If I were twenty years younger, I would settle here. . . . I want to see Florida, also.

Booth was homeless, a wanderer; his wives, his mother, were gone. Now he conceived of an idea for a special club in New York for actors, artists, writers, all men of feeling and importance in the cultural world of the city. The plan was brilliantly executed. The famous architect, Stanford White, designed the four-story building of high ceilings and inviting fireplaces. The dining room and bar, models of exquisite taste, rang to the chatter of gifted men for the first time on New Year's Eve, 1888.

Edwina herself shipped a pine log down from Boston for their fire. "Gentlemen," Edwin raised his glass, "let us fire the yule log, with the request that it be burnt as her offering of love, peace and good will to the Players . . ."

His voice broke.

He wrote to Edwina, "I cannot describe the universal joy which pervaded all hearts present, the sympathy expressed, the entire success of everything."

Explaining the Players Club, Booth wrote a friend that it was "for the ultimate benefit of actors," to serve as a beacon to the "poor player"— to lift him above the Bohemian level.

The years would pass.

But he must continue to act. "You know," he wrote Edwina, "I have acted *Hamlet* for many years, and many hundred times. Well, I am just learning many things that were hidden all this while in the obscurity of its wonderful depths of thought; so, when you are 365 years old, you will give up guessing."

He toured, relentlessly optimistic. This from Kansas City:

> Yours of 21st, forwarded from Chicago, came yesterday. . . . I told you in my last that the theatre here was roofless, and otherwise unfit for use. It was little better Tuesday night. At nine o'clock at night there were fifty workmen removing lumber, driving nails and doing all sorts of work, amid a perfect whirlwind of noise, and freezing blasts of wind. At ten o'clock a half scene and a red sheet were drawn aside, and the play, *Othello,* began, to about seventy-five people in hats, overcoats and heavy fur wraps, most of whom left as the play progressed, unable to endure the cold. Not a door was in the place, and the sky was in full view above the auditorium and part of the stage. . . . Last night we had some stoves, a tarpaulin cover for a roof, several scenes, and played . . . to about two hundred people. . . . The hotel we are at is not much better, but a warm wave is on, and I keep well and take care of my bones.

When Booth played in San Francisco in 1889, returning to the scenes of his youthful acting opposite Catherine Sinclair and Laura Keene before gold-rush audiences, his health broke. But he wrote his daughter none of this:

> The weather here has been about the same as yours, except that instead of a cyclone, we had an earthquake—the first genuine shock I ever felt, and the worst, it is said, since 1868, when a very severe one did great damage. Strange to say, this one so unusually violent, and of such long duration, did no damage whatever.

But to an old friend, who had been with him in the early California days, he said, "I could *act* then, had all the enthusiasm of youth . . . yet I couldn't convince the people I was a good actor. I am now old and they are paying five and ten dollars a seat, and I cannot act at all."

In Rochester, in 1889, he lost his voice. The audience, amazed, filed contentedly out, pleased at least at having witnessed a historic occasion.

He continued to live at the Players Club, in the apartment on the upper floor. A huge brass canopied bed. A dresser on which rested two skulls used in Hamlet. Closets of precious costumes. Here, at an inlaid secretary desk, he wrote to his daughter letters which became shorter with time.

November 17, 1889: "It is not possible for me to remember anything. I thought you were to dine out today. I have slept nearly all the time . . . wish I had some of your beef and cabbage."

Then he grew well. John Singer Sargent painted his portrait in oils for the club. He returned to the theater, steady as ever:

> Many folk, chiefly women and girls, come on from Washington to see the play, and stop over night; Friday night this house was full of 'em, and when I came here after the play about thirty of them were in the hall in double lines, through which I had to pass. . . . Demands for my autograph . . . were numerous.

In a letter dated April 10, 1890, a fascinating note on the inventions of the times:

> I received your "wire-gram" last night and your "phonogram" just now. I wired you three cheers for [your son's birthday]. I'll try to unwind the cylinder tomorrow.

So the Edison phonograph cylinders were being mailed in lieu of letters.

Four days later, Booth played Detroit:

> After the play Saturday I took the train, and had a sleepless night. . . . Arrived at 9 A.M. so tired that I slept off and on nearly all day. At eight o'clock last night, as I was about to write you, a fire broke out in the Plankinton Hotel, just across a narrow street from this one and quite near the theatre. . . . The immense crowd of people, and the noise and the sparks of the engines all about the house till eleven o'clock, upset my efforts to write. I got ready what valuables I have with me, expecting this house to take fire, but by midnight, all was quiet.
>
> Yes; it is indeed most gratifying to feel that age has not rendered my work stale and tiresome, as is usually the case with actors. . . . Your dear mother's fear was that I would culminate too early, as I seemed then to be advancing so rapidly. . . . But as for the compensation, nothing of fame or fortune can compensate for the spiritual suffering that one possessing such qualities has to endure. To pass life in a sort of dream, where "Nothing is but what is not" a loneliness in the very midst of a constant crowd, as it were, is not a desirable condition of existence, especially when the body also has to share the "penalty of greatness," as it is

termed. . . . I'd rather be an obscure farmer, a hayseed from way back, or a cabinetmaker, as my father advised, than the most distinguished man on earth.

In the spring of 1891, he gave his last performances, in *Hamlet*. Crowds thronged to hear him, for this obviously was the great Booth at his end, who might never be seen again.

"I am not saying good-by for good," he said afterward to the audience. "I intend to rest next year for the benefit of my health and I expect to appear before you in the near future. Again I thank you—and I hope it will not be for the last time."

Bromely, a manager who knew him well, said, "Booth at fifty-eight is older than many a man of seventy."

Otis Skinner, who was to become famous, later wrote, "Ten years had dug devitalizing claws into his great strength, his spirit and his ambition. It was the shell of the great actor, old and tired and unhappy."

Booth saw his daughter often; when he did not, he wrote.

On February 26, 1893, she received this letter from the Players:

> Again it seems as tho' a year has passed since I wrote to you, so long a time it seems; but I can't complain of your silence or neglect of me, for you have been very prompt, and every now and then I receive your welcome letters, darling, which make me very happy in my gloomy club room; for I seldom go out or downstairs, keeping upstairs nearly all the time. Have been only to Daly's, and shall go again there and see the *Twelfth Night* on Tuesday. . . . There is a great Italian actress here, a Mlle. Duse, the greatest yet, they say. I shall see her in a few nights.

But often, though he planned, he did not go out. When he did, he could be found in his private box, head sensitively inclined as he listened, with some difficulty, to the young actor reading Shakespeare below.

"His eyes," said a friend, "retain their marvelous beauty, like a lamp burning in a deserted temple."

On Tuesday, April 17, 1893, he dined with his daughter, despite a headache. That night he read himself to sleep; poetry. He was found in the morning, the book open, unconscious.

Booth had suffered a stroke, a hemorrhaging of a blood vessel in the brain. But he did not die. Paralyzed in the right side, he clung to life.

Edwina wrote, "I longed ever to be with him, not knowing how much longer I might have that happiness."

She was beside him constantly. She brought his grandchildren.

"How are you, dear Grandpa?" they asked.

"How are you yourself, old fellow?" he would answer cheerfully.

On June 7, a night of hard rain and thunder, he had a relapse. He gasped for breath. The lights went out. "Don't let father die in the dark!" Edwina cried. Candles were brought. But the lights came on again.

"It was like the passing of a shadow," said the doctor afterward, for the change in him had been so little. The physician walked to the window and as a signal waved a white handkerchief. Reporters waiting below rushed off to write their flowery obituaries. Next morning, from coast to coast, the life of this actor and the deeds of his infamous brother were discussed.

On the morning of June 9, Booth's body was carried from the Players to church, then toward the cemetery. While the cortege was in progress, fate arranged a most peculiar finale to this unusual life story.

In Washington, Ford's Theatre collapsed. By then an office building, it killed twenty-two workers in the wreckage; fifty more were injured.

It was as though John Wilkes Booth in hell, rampaging over Edwin's death, had pulled some terrible chain, and set the capital trembling again, as he had thirty years before.

7
James O'Neill:
The Count of Monte Cristo

EDWIN BOOTH was at the height of his popularity when he returned to Chicago in 1872 to star with McVicker's stock company at McVicker's Theatre, outclassed only by Mrs. Drew's Arch Street Theatre, Philadelphia, and Wallack's in New York. Audiences flocked to see him, eager to forget the trials and tribulations of the recent and terrible fire.

Edwin Booth, at thirty-nine, was near the zenith of his powers as an actor. Proud of his abilities and secure in his position as leading American male star, he looked forward to a rather relaxed and uncontentious series of performances as he walked streets turbulent with the massive wave of reconstruction then sweeping the ever-optimistic city. As he entered Chicago by rail that night, a vast blackness met his eyes where once rows of cheery streetlamps and the window lights of homes provided welcome. Instead, he saw only bobbling carriage lanterns against the nothingness. Depressed, he was reassured by J. H. McVicker's words that the city was coming back, and audiences too. Nothing could stop Chicago; she was the crossroads of America. Most assuring was McVicker's description of the stock company—all oiled silk in the slickness of its acting.

"We have a leading man in a million," said McVicker when Booth met him for dinner at the hotel. "His name is James O'Neill, an Irishman, arrived in America at an early age, and his brogue well on the mend. As handsome as a prince. The voice of an angel." Booth frowned slightly. "Trouble yourself not, Edwin," added the older man. "His prime is not on him, he will not detract from you—but even Forrest has had strong words for him. O'Neill is a man to watch. Teach him, help him."

Such advice was wasted, for it was unnecessary. Booth realized this the moment he laid eyes on the young O'Neill. There was in him a vigor, directness, and magnetism he had not seen in an actor in some time.

"Well, you are my Iago," Booth said. "And I your Othello."

O'Neill hesitated, then simply nodded. He stood in terrible awe of this figure; yet his confidence was unshaken. Of far lesser reputation at twenty-five, he was nonetheless well seasoned, and encouraged to that dream of greatness which in time may rob a man of sanity.

The two removed their coats, their ties, opened their collars, stood slack and relaxed, then moved easily into rehearsal. The air snapped to the meter of their poetry. All stood back marveling at the counterpoint provided by O'Neill to Booth's affecting Othello.

During a scene in which Booth did not perform, he found himself standing with the theater manager.

"He *is* good," said the manager. "The public has a watch on him, we've seen that the past weeks here. They'll decide who to worship and who not to."

"That man is playing the part better than I ever did," mused Booth.

Later, the manager quoted Booth to O'Neill in order to encourage him. O'Neill ran his fingers into his hair as a look of blank amazement swept his face. "Please," he said, "would you have Mr. Booth write that down for me."

At first the request seemed absurd, but recalling the little he knew of O'Neill's hard times, he decided he understood the request. Confident as young Jimmy seemed, he keenly felt the hollowness of his poor past, as though his modest success might fly before the winds of chance.

Some time later, the manager handed O'Neill a slip of paper bearing Booth's statement and signed by the great man. All his life he carried that paper in his wallet over his heart. Proud though it made him, he would live to read it with remorse, remembering how, in glorious days, they had called him "the new Booth."

O'Neill became the sensation of the 1870's, a mysterious, dashing figure who played to standing room in Chicago, trading roles with Booth night by night. Touring, he acted opposite the gargantuan Charlotte Cushman and other fine stars, none of whom found him wanting.

Critics and actors alike wondered at the music and color of his voice; during his most promising years he was to be known professionally as "The Voice."

O'Neill's success unloosed a voluble tongue. He became his own best press agent.

"It was Kilkenny—smiling Kilkenny—where I was born one opal-tinted day in October, 1847," he told reporters, shaving a bit from his age. "Were I permitted to choose a birthplace for any Irishman's child, be he dreamy-eyed son of Erin with star fire in his heart, or laughing gossoon with song on his lip and roguery in his eye, 't would be that same little town in old Leinster."

His eyes twinkled while their pencils flew.

O'Neill omitted the fact that his father Edward had been a poor man, whose scrap of land under the shadow of Strongbow's castle could scarcely support eight children. When potatoes throughout the country became blighted, a starving population fell prey to epidemic typhus. Sadly, Edward and Mary Ann took their children and joined the massive migration which was proceeding from the land to the port of Queenstown and onto any hulk that would take them aboard.

While gulls swerved overhead, the fugitives stood in a queue. It was steerage for them: calling in the dimness to some they knew, hearing the crack of hard bread in the dark or the cough and spit of sick children. Curled in a great coil of rope, five-year-old Jimmy O'Neill fell asleep to the creaking of the old timbered ship.

In due course, little James O'Neill saw the port of New York, which was simpler then, unadorned by bridges or the Statue of Liberty to welcome him. The O'Neills were speedily processed through what Customs and medical checks there were. Immigrant labor met an open hand and was readily assimilated.

It did not go well for Edward O'Neill in the boisterous city. He could not find work in the machinist's trade. The family moved on to Buffalo, where the glories of the Falls did nothing to relieve their want. There Edward labored long hours in a shop so drafty that the man operating the forge was envied for his job. Chilled and exhausted, O'Neill fought his way home at night against the Lake Erie wind to a house no more than a shack. Little Jimmy and his five younger sisters would have been long asleep.

Edward was a thin man, with the leathery, hollow, worker's chest, and hand calluses hard as wood. He would sit silent, grinding his teeth, thinking of the wasted day. Mary Ann would give him tea, rich with herbs to help the cough he suffered during the second winter.

One night, hacking miserably, he brought up blood. He was as good as dead as far as he was concerned.

Among these poor, who were derisively called "bog Irish" by those who spoke without a brogue, it was believed that "the consumption" must be fatal. "I'm to die," said O'Neill, "and I'll do that in Ireland." Without much thought for anyone else, he booked passage alone for Queenstown.

James—now the eldest resident son, two brothers having left—found himself forced to support the family. At ten he became a clerk, then a machinist's apprentice—twelve hours a day, six days a week. He was paid fifty cents a week, which bought a considerable amount of rough food, not much else.

James's luck turned when his eldest sister married a successful Norfolk, Virginia, clothing store manager, who not only sent money to his mother-in-law, but agreed to take the boy under his wing.

At fourteen, James O'Neill exchanged sledgehammers, files, and cold chisels for tape measure, marking chalk, and needles. Instead of the drafty, dirty machine-shop shed, there was a comfortable, carpeted haberdashery where he learned to sew Confederate soldiers' uniforms and to stitch on the chevrons of promotion.

There were books now in his home, and in the evenings, a chance to attend a play, either Shakespeare or some popular comedy. In the rhythms of poetry and dramatic lines, read aloud to him by his sister or heard on the stage, he found an excitement, a lilt, a rhythm, which he echoed in a colorful brogue.

The Civil War ended, and with it James's stay in Norfolk. He went north to Cincinnati, where his family had moved. For a while he worked for low wages as a maker of files. At night he played billiards at the National Saloon where stage people spent spare time. At nineteen, he was good-looking, straight and athletic, with a manly bearing and an ease of motion almost liquid. White teeth flashed in a smile that might have seemed automatic even then, and the gaze from his eyes, black and gay, was returned with pleasure. He rather overpowered the ladies.

One night O'Neill looked up from a rack of balls to hear the manager of the National Theatre recruiting extras among the sporting crowd. O'Neill rushed forward.

He remembered in later years the velvet breeches, satin embroidered coat, ruffles, and knee buckles he had worn, and how he had carried a spear while he marched behind famous Edwin Forrest.

Later, he was occasionally given a line to speak. "There was a ringing in my ears," he told his pals subsequently, "and a sensation of drowning in deep waters swept across my heart."

With the years, O'Neill could not retell a story without some embellishment, compounding whatever series of embellishments had preceded. His friends knew that his most hilarious anecdote smelled of imagination. "Once the dialogue between the leading woman and the heavy man was somewhat spirited, and finally it led up to a situation where she confessed her love for him, which he refused. I had my own ideas of chivalry," he declared, "and possibly my high regard and respect for the weaker sex caused me to jump into the breach. Having forgotten for a moment where I was, I said to her: 'I'll take you! He's no good anyway!' "

According to O'Neill, the audience roared, and he stumbled offstage to be met by the cheers and laughter of the actors. The stage manager was furious. "You're all laughing at me now," O'Neill remembered saying, "because you think I made an ass of myself. I'm going to be an actor; I'm going to be a *star;* and you'll be coming to me some day asking for a position under me, and then the laugh will be on the other side of your face."

Those closest to young O'Neill knew the story had basis in the fact that he could not speak a line without revealing his heavy accent. For that, he may have been ridiculed to the point of declaring extreme ambition.

O'Neill was tenacious, which was plainer to no one than Pop Seaman, a run-down old actor with the troupe, who took O'Neill under his wing, gave him acting lessons, and kept him in steady work as a "super" at 25 cents a show.

For three years, Pop and Jimmy toured the Midwest, bumming meals, often stranded by bankrupt stage companies, hitching rides, and fighting landladies who had seized their possessions in lieu of rent.

In this hard school O'Neill learned rapidly.

Within a year, he was playing juvenile roles. A year later, he had second male leads. A year after that, he was leading man at Ellsler's Academy of Music, Cleveland, on Johnson Street—and Pop was serving as his "dresser."

Pop's full name was Alfred Hamilton Seaman; he had ambitions too.

"Now you've got money, Jimmy," he said kindly one night, "why don't you set me up in something for my old age—a little business."

"All right," said O'Neill, "what's your line?"

Soon Pop Seaman was sporting a business card: "Alfred H. Seaman, Theatrical Costumes." James eventually broke with A. H. Seaman. He toured with the lovely Louise Hawthorne in Uncle Dick Hooley's *Parlor Home of Comedy*.

Illustrious and fairly well paid, James O'Neill found his climb blocked by his brogue, which was particularly objectionable in Shakespearean acting. Attending rehearsals of the great stars, he noted their style and mimicked their elocution. However, in the heat of emotion, his beautiful voice betrayed his origin.

Then came a chance to support the popular Joseph Jefferson in a minor part. After the play, Jefferson sent for him. "My boy," he said, "you got six rounds of applause tonight, and that is good." O'Neill held his breath. "But there are *eight* rounds in the part, and we must get them."

Two performances later, O'Neill got them all.

He impressed everyone with his doggedness.

O'Neill may have understood the necessity for cleansing his speech of accent; he cannot have appreciated being asked to salvage and embellish that brogue in *Rip Van Winkle*. Nor can he have had much patience with the attitude of "Americans" toward "foreigners," "papists," and "shanty Irish." Jefferson, seventeen years his senior, and a third-generation actor, understood his frustration and commiserated with him. O'Neill listened to stories of "real hardship" from the veteran.

Joe had debuted at three, in 1832. He had painted scenery as a child, he said, and sold tickets. He acted with his mother on a stage of boards thrown across a pigsty, while the pigs squealed below. These and other hardships of a family of strolling players on the frontier amused O'Neill. He in turn was moved by the plight of talented Negroes who, according to Jefferson, had far less chance of finding a rightful place on the stage than did he, an Irishman.

To prove his point, Jefferson told about the birth of the minstrel show, a blackface semimusical given by white men in mimicry and caricature of black men, who were not permitted to portray themselves. The minstrel form had been started by white Thomas D. Rice, who played a Kentucky cornfield hand in *The Rifle*. To liven the part he added a shuffling dance and song done by an old slave he had watched in a marketplace:

> Wheel about, turn about
>   Do jis so,
> And ebery time I wheel about
>   I jump Jim Crow.

These blackface shows, popular in Europe as well as in America, said Jefferson, were ample reminder to the Irish of what difficulties lay ahead in a free country for a people recently freed.

"Why, in London, playing there," laughed Jefferson, "I saw chimney sweeps in sooty faces doing Jim Crow dances and songs as they hauled their brush carts down the streets. When I was a tiny child, they black-faced me and put me in a sack. On cue, I tumbled out following Rice's big song and did my own takeoff on 'Wheel About, Turn About.' Now that you've a bit of Irish character-playing to do in *Rip,* you would think it was world's end."

O'Neill shrugged. Jefferson had more than made his point. He had but to consider the career of Ira Frederick Aldridge, which was then well known, to appreciate his relative good fortune. Born black in New York in 1804, Aldridge was educated at a Negro school, where he showed un-common dramatic talent that carried him to the segregated African Theatre. Enthusiastically encouraged by some whites, he nevertheless found himself barred from theaters in every major city. Aldridge sailed to London, where he met ridicule and opposition in lesser degree. Like O'Neill, his principal ambition had been Shakespeare. Aldridge's rendi-tions of Othello, Lear, and Macbeth were superb, and his acclaim stormy. He received tributes from kings, was honored in Russia, and built a for-tune in Europe, where he died in 1867. An attempt to return to the United States had failed. With his death and the liberation of American blacks, the ghost of Aldridge passed into the consciences of some American actors.

Two years after Aldridge's death O'Neill vowed that he himself would perform a masterful Othello, Lear, Romeo, and Hamlet. Edwin Booth had become his idol. Whenever he could he bought admission where Booth was playing. So intense was his fixation that he could not believe his eyes when McVicker wired him an offer to join the Chicago stock company with which Booth would appear.

One Chicago critic disapproved of Booth's influence on the impression-able O'Neill: "Most of all did he become the pattern of Edwin Booth. So keenly did he study Booth that he copied even his defects in mannerisms. He dressed like him, posed like him, and finally came to speak like him."

O'Neill was warned that he must develop a style of his own. Concen-tration on his brogue distracted him from that purpose; delight in the sheer excitement of flamboyant acting delayed serious study and self-ex-

Ira Aldridge, as Aaron in *Titus Andronicus,* 1852. A Negro actor born in America, he won fame abroad for his Shakespearean roles. Engraving of a daguerreotype

amination. Why worry when one could read such reports as this: "The house was packed to the doors when Macduff announced the foul murder, the curtain went down on a roar of applause, which continued until Mr. Booth stepped before the curtain—when all at once, the applause ceased. Mr. Booth walked across the stage from left to right and disappeared. Then the applause was renewed in tones of thunder. Men and women stood up, waving their handkerchiefs and crying, 'O'Neill, O'Neill!' This applause and shouting were deafening. O'Neill came before the footlights, blushing like a boy."

O'Neill was given the role of Romeo to play opposite Adelaide Nielson, an English actress described as the most beautiful Juliet who ever lived. In the scene in which Juliet finds Romeo dead, he kissed her full upon the mouth.

"How could you? How could you?" she demanded later. James pointed out jovially that, being dead, he could not have kissed her, but that her Juliet would bring anyone back to life. Years later, Nielson said, "The greatest Romeo I ever played with was a curly-haired Irishman. When I played with other Romeos, I thought they would climb up the trellis to the balcony; but when I played with Jimmy O'Neill, I wanted to climb down the trellis, into his arms."

O'Neill joined the troupe of Richard Hooley, won a raise in salary, and played Hamlet, Shylock, and other great roles. He stormed San Francisco in 1875, to find show business there as lucrative and sophisticated as it had been in Chicago. In every city he had his way with the ladies. He departed after two months, sent off by a grand farewell benefit.

The man who waved his hat in San Francisco was not the boy who had trembled beside Booth in Chicago. Among the heavy-spending silver miners fresh from the Comstock Lode in nearby Nevada, O'Neill felt a very big man. It was not a modest and shivering protégé who returned to Cleveland to pursue the hand of Mary Ellen Quinlan.

O'Neill had known her in 1871 and 1872 when he had played Cleveland with Ellsler's company; she was only fifteen then; he had known her father Thomas, a wealthy businessman, now deceased, who had bequeathed to quiet, mystical Ella a large estate.

Like so many men who have lived high and fast, James O'Neill was attracted by Ella's purity. And despite many escapades, he was a religious man who admired in Ella her piety. She had excelled at convent school— St. Mary's Academy, in Notre Dame, Indiana, from which she was graduated with honors in music—and for a time she had considered becoming a nun. James was subtly fascinated by her having attended the school which had graduated Edwin Booth's second wife seven years before.

Ella Quinlan's resistance to O'Neill was not great. It was her mother who fought Ella's involvement with the notorious actor. After all, Ella Quinlan admitted she had fallen in love with James five years before, at the age of fifteen, when her father took her to see James play *A Tale of Two Cities,* and that was that.

Their romance flowered. Soon Ella Quinlan was visiting New York, a thousand dollars in her purse, to buy her trousseau. Along Broadway, from Ninth to Twentieth, in an area called "The Ladies' Mile," Ella shopped at Macy's, Lord & Taylor, Arnold Constable, and A. T. Stewart's. Fourteenth Street was uptown. On Union Square, Tiffany & Co. showed its wares to James O'Neill, who needed a diamond ring.

James appeared in New York in *The Two Orphans,* an agonizing story including a simulated snowstorm, in which honor triumphed over villainy. Watching from her box, Ella Quinlan blushed with pride.

O'Neill's manager sent *The Two Orphans* across the East River to the Brooklyn Theatre, and O'Neill might have gone, had not his popularity held him in Manhattan, where he was cast in *Miss Multon* at the Union Square Theatre. On December 5, the Brooklyn Theatre burned; 295, many of them actors, died in that fire.

On July 14 of the following year, 1875, Ella and James were married.

On September 28, 1878, James O'Neill, Jr., was born to the couple. The proud father, dreading the loneliness of tours, insisted that his wife and child join him as soon as possible. Ella complied, and they stayed at family hotels.

O'Neill's popularity continued, and his mastery of difficult roles increased. One day he was offered the role of Christ in a play titled *The Passion.* Discussions with the promoters convinced him of their good intentions, and it was over the moral objections of Ella and others close to him that he agreed to open the play at the Baldwin Theatre, San Francisco, as an act of worship to Jesus.

So intense was his performance that women in the audience fell to their knees. During the crowning with thorns, many people fainted.

Young David Belasco brought such realism to the production—he used an actual herd of sheep, a group of nursing mothers and babies—that the play was vividly convincing. James O'Neill took his final curtain in relative silence. The ordinary bustle of a departing audience was replaced by a seething sound of voices, querulous and ominous.

There were many Irish in the theater, people of intense belief. So moved were some, enflamed by the crucifixion, that once outside they formed a mob, and roving the city, attacked Jews and smashed their shops.

A Protestant faction raised another issue. James had impersonated Christ; threats arrived as the play continued; he must stop or they would beat him within an inch of his life.

The city banned the play.

O'Neill returned to New York and began a struggle to reopen the play. "If the public will support me," he insisted, "I shall devote the remainder of my life to this great work. I have no desire to go back to the routine work of the stage at all. I believe I can do more good by this presentation than any of the ministers from their pulpits." Armed with hundreds of letters from people who had been inspired by the play, O'Neill persuaded Henry Abbey to mount a new production. Again, turmoil forced a closing.

O'Neill felt rebuffed; his motives had been questioned. In intimate conversation he revealed his preoccupation with rightness and goodness. He had wished only to purvey the message of Christ, he defended, and if a religious or morality play were a method for doing that, why not do that? He would not listen to suggestions that perhaps he had done so in a rather broad and melodramatic manner.

O'Neill's next venture, *An American King,* cost him three years' work, ended in failure, and took him almost irretrievably from the Shakespeare he had professed to love.

Clearly, O'Neill had decided that to enjoy a large income and self-satisfaction he ought to have a play of his own, a characterization with which to become identified. For a time he searched for such a vehicle; then a producer's necessity brought him a thin opportunity, one that developed into a gold mine and completed his artistic downfall.

Alexandre Dumas' immense and immensely successful novel, *The Count of Monte Cristo,* had been published in France in 1845. Dumas' dramatization, *Monte Cristo,* faithful to his own every word, had required 20 acts, 37 tableaux or panoramic sets, 221 scenes, and 59 characters.

When this was attempted at the Drury Lane, London, in 1848, patrons tore up the benches, and became, as one observer put it, "a howling mob."

Twenty years later, an abbreviated version by Charles Fechter failed, as had various other attempts since 1848. Fechter pursued his ambition to adapt the stirring novel as relentlessly as Edmond Dantès, hero of the play, struggled for revenge against the man who imprisoned him for fourteen years. Many versions later, playwright Fechter died penniless.

John Stetson, proprietor of the Globe Theatre, Boston, inherited the final Fechter script in 1883, and decided to play it in New York, at Booth's Theatre, with James O'Neill as Dantès, on February 12.

O'Neill succeeded in getting himself snowbound, turned up unrehearsed and delivered the part coarsely. His movements were graceful, however, and his swordsmanship superb. In a grand scene, Dantès is flung from a castle wall, tied in a sack—with a large cannonball for company—and falls among cleverly contrived canvas waves which workmen offstage cause to billow realistically.

"An ugly night on the sea," says the first jailer.

"Aye, under, too," says the second as they make their exit.

The sack, of course, contained something bulky and light. Under the fake waves, wet and sprinkled with salt which would glitter, O'Neill waited for his moment of triumphant emergence. He must have pictured Dantès writhing in the sack attempting to extricate his knife, his lungs bursting, then the knife in his hand, slashing, slashing, swimming out.

The audience waited, holding its collective breath.

Above the stage the moon came out, the moon of good fortune.

Here came the dripping O'Neill, struggling onto the rocks, shreds of sack cemented to the blade of his knife.

"Saved!" he shouted. "Mine, the treasures of Monte Cristo! The world is mine!"

The audience went wild.

In New York, *Spirit of the Times* said, "The revival of *Monte Cristo* was a failure, and . . . it deserved to fail. . . . Mr. O'Neill is an actor with an Irish name and an Irish accent but without any Irish sympathy, passion or magnetism."

The New York Times disagreed: "Mr. O'Neill failed to make an impression of strength because he applied to broad and dashing romantic acting the restrained method of realism. His intensity at the closing scenes of the play was, nevertheless, dramatic and somewhat magnetic."

O'Neill for the first time properly rehearsed the play. Again and again

Week Beginning Monday, January 6, 1902.

Regular Matinees Wednesdays and Saturdays

Liebler & Co.'s Great Organization, Supporting

Mr. James O'Neill

In Charles Fechter's Version of Dumas' Masterpiece,

"MONTE CRISTO"

CAST OF CHARACTERS.

EDMOND DANTES	MR. JAMES O NEILL
NORTIER	FREDERIC DE BELLEVILLE
ALBERT DE MORCERF	JAMES O'NEILL, JR.
VILLEFORTE	WARREN CONLAN
CADEROUSSE	W. J. DIXON
FERNAND	CLAUDE GILBERT
MOREL	EDWARD LALLY
DANGLARS	JOSEPH SLAYTOR
ABBA FARIA	MARK ELLSWORTH
OLD DANTES	EDWARD THOMAS
PENELON	HARRY LAPPIN
GOVERNOR OF PRISON	R. J. CLOUD
COMMISSARY	CHARLES LELAND
GERMAIN	JOHN GREEN
BRIGADIER	JAS. BEEBE
1st GAOLER	ED. BOUCHARD
2d GAOLER	ED. SMITH
1st POLICE AGENT	JAMES C. HUNTER
2d POLICE AGENT	ALBERT CLARK
SENTINEL	FRED LUCE
SERVANT	LEON GORDON
MAN	THOS. DALE
FISHERMAN	ROBT. AYRE
MERCEDES	MISS SELENE JOHNSON
CARCONTE	KATE FLETCHER
MLLE. DANGLARS	VIRGINIA KEATING
WOMAN	REBECCA HOCK

Catalans, Ship's Crew, Fisherman, Gendarms, Guests, Waiters, Servants.

SCENIC SYNOPSIS.

ACT I.—Scene 1—The Port of Marseilles. (Ernest Gros.) Scene 2—Villeforte's Cabinet. (Ernest Gros.) Scene 3—The Reserve Inn. (Ernest Gros.) A lapse of eighteen years between Act I and Act II.

ACT II.—Scene 1—Hall in Hotel de Morcerf. (John H. Young.) Scene 2—The Prison of the Chateau d If. (John H. Young.) Scene 3—The Open Sea. (John H. Young.)

ACT III.—Scene—Inn of the Pont du Gard. (Gates & Morange.)

ACT IV.—Scene—Conservatory and Ballroom in Hotel de Morcerf. (Ernest Albert.)

ACT V.—Scene—Forest of Fontainebleu. (Homer Emmens.)

Playbill of O'Neill's *Monte Cristo,* January 6, 1902

Dantès emerged from the waves. Audiences grew; bookings piled up, and the critics, if unimpressed by the play itself, agreed that James O'Neill was thrilling.

Monte Cristo was not without its moments of eloquence, as in the "excuse" speech in which Dantès attempts to extricate himself from unwitting involvement in a plot to restore Emperor Napoleon to the leadership of France.

Villefort listens, with a kindly expression, unaware that Dantès in his innocence, in accidental complicity informed of the strategy against the king, will soon know who the actual conspirators are. Villefort is one of them.

The audiences of that day hunched on the edge of their seats, keening their ears to catch each detail of unfolding suspense as O'Neill's mellifluous words rolled forth:

> EDMOND: It is true that I arrived from Smyrna, it is true that I cast anchor at Elba, it is true that I received a letter from the emperor's hand, but I was ignorant of any plot. . . .
>
> VILLEFORT: Yet, you went out of your course to touch at Elba; you therefore called there expressly of your own will, in the teeth of your owner's orders. This bears a very serious appearance.
>
> EDMOND: I see too well it does, but it was not of my own doing . . . on leaving Naples, where I believe he had an interview with Murat, our captain fell ill of brainfever. He grew rapidly worse, and feeling himself dying and his senses about to desert him, he called me to his side. "Dantès," he said, "swear to me by your honor as a sailor, by your faith in Heaven, by your love of me, to discharge when I am gone, the mission I shall confide to you, and with which I was entrusted. Do not hesitate, my body's rest, my soul's salvation, my honor are at stake!"— and the tears coursed down his bronzed and burning cheek. I could demur no longer. I swore. Then, with his ring, he gave me a packet, commanded me to steer for the Island of Elba. To land at Port Farrajo, to have the ring conveyed to the emperor and to place the packet in his own hands. In a few moments he was dead. I reached Elba. I had the ring conveyed to the emperor—I gave him the packet. He entrusted me with a letter which a stranger he described would ask me for on landing at Marseilles. As soon as I arrived, the stranger presented himself, and I was on my way to get the letter, left in my cabin, when I was arrested.

The audience held its breath. Now, Dantès, destined for prison, counthood, and revenge, would deliver his heart's declaration:

EDMOND: This is the truth, the whole truth, by my honor as a sailor, by my love for Mercedes, by my father's life!
VILLEFORT: Yes, I believe you. You are surely innocent.

Cheers from the gallery.

EDMOND: Thanks, monsieur, adieu, and thanks.
VILLEFORT: Where are you going?
EDMOND: I am going away.
VILLEFORT: But you are not free yet.
EDMOND: You say I am innocent—how are the guilty treated?
VILLEFORT: That is just what you and I are going to consider.

Hisses from the gallery.
Later, the blow falls:

VILLEFORT: Arrest him—let him be conveyed at once to the dungeons of the Chateau d'If and be kept in strict and most careful detention . . . the mouth of the young sailor sealed, no trace remains of the pernicious secret.

So the audience groaned and bit its nails.

Nightly at the theater, ragged and bearded, O'Neill did the prison scene, so revealing of the play's simple power:

EDMOND: Only the thickness of one stone between us and the sky! Between us and liberty! I can hear the tread of the sentinel above.
FARIA: So that by detaching one or two stones—
EDMOND: The stone falls! And if we can seize the precise moment when the sentinel passes, he falls with it, too, we gag him, bind him fast, both climb through the aperture, and before they are up to change the guard, we shall have swum the coast and be free. Where are the ropes and the gag?
FARIA: There, under my bed!
EDMOND: Liberty at last!
FARIA: Yes, at last! After eighteen years of struggle, of incessant toil. Never shall I forget the patience, the devotion you brought to this rough task, when my enfeebled limbs were powerless to assist you. From this day forth, Edmond, you are my son, my heir.
EDMOND: My father!
FARIA: Think not it is an idle word. . . . I have often in our conversation dwelt upon the history of the Borgias, have I not? You remember the poisons by whose agency they made themselves heirs of the cardinals who died around them. My ancestor, Cardinal Spada, of whom I

am the last descendant, was one of their victims. But, knowing them of old, he had buried his treasure in a place unknown to that age, and of which he was the proprietor—the Island of Monte Cristo. Therefore, when the hour of his death arrived, when the Borgias came to search out his immense and renowned treasure, nothing was found in his palace. No gold, no jewels, nothing but an old breviary, in which was written "to my heirs."

EDMOND: Well?

FARIA: Well, its trifling value rendered its sale worthless, this worn old breviary remained in our family, and at last the book fell to me, and for years, I used to turn over the pages again and again—convinced that the breviary contained the mystery of the missing treasure. Finally one evening, feeling that the book was driving me mad, I flung it into the fire. The page on which the words were written was its first page, and the flames which had already seized upon the remainder of the book, made it radiate to my eyes, some other characters appeared upon the surface. I snatched the page from the fire and read, written in a sympathetic ink which at once became visible on exposure to strong heat, these lines—"Fearing from my knowledge of the Borgias, that they hope by my poisoning to secure my fortune speedily, I hid all that I possess in ingots, coined money, jewels, diamonds and trinkets, in the secret grottoes of my Island of Monte Cristo. This treasure will be found on raising the twentieth rock, counting in a straight line from the little creek, eastward, and I bequeath it to my heirs.

EDMOND: This is a fairy tale!

FARIA: Here is the page, Edmond, it is a reality!

Faria bequeathes his secret, and dies of exhaustion. Dantès, having hidden in Faria's shroud, is thrown in his place into the sea, and escapes. He seizes the fortune, and his revenge. His enemies die—there are three. As each falls, in separate actions, Dantès counts: "One—two—three!" So popular was the play becoming that the call, "One—two—three!" became synonymous in daily language for revenge, or, "Look out!" The saying, "The world is mine," also became good for a laugh from one coast to the other.

In life, O'Neill failed to find the world he wanted—he did search for more treasure. Investing widely in property, he sustained large losses and made few gains. He fought to protect the exclusive rights to his play, even going to the state supreme court, because rival companies attempted to tour in mutilated versions.

One troupe brought out a sequel, *The Son of Monte Cristo.*

Another did a parody, *Monte Cristo, Jr.*

The country was mad for Monte Cristo, the poor man done in, become rich and royal. It was our story, the story of our country, and the fantasy fate of many in it.

Bored, working and traveling, O'Neill drank perhaps too much. One night he had trouble rising above the waves, and the audience had to wait patiently, perhaps assuming that for once the sack had proved too strong or his knife too dull.

Finally he emerged and staggered, gasping softly, to his well-worn wooden rock. "The world is mine!" he said uneasily. It most assuredly was not. This was altogether clear in the way lesser actors treated him. Ella remained at home, her second child expected. On the road, James brooded and drank. In his boredom he took to the bars after each performance. "On Monte Cristo," he would shout, slapping the wood, and the men would come around, strangers, to grab their glasses. "On Monte Cristo," they would echo. "Here's to the Count of Monte Cristo."

Gradually, O'Neill had fused with the character Edmond Dantès. Why not? In its first year, *Monte Cristo* had netted $50,000.

Playing in San Francisco, O'Neill excited the critic for the *News Letter,* who said, "The apotheosis of this absurdity is the scene where Dantès, standing on a two-by-four rock in the midst of bobbing chunks of wood and canvas, received a shower of salt. That this play, with all these supremely ridiculous details . . . should still . . . amuse, is a proof of its strong romantic interest and powerful dramatic force. It is bound to draw for some time."

James played on the guarantee of $1,000 a week and a share in the box-office receipts.

Offers to book *Cristo* were wired in from every major city.

Ella gave birth to a second son—whom James named Edmund Burke O'Neill, after a Dublin-born English statesman, he claimed. Many thought the coincidence too much and were reminded that Dantès' first name was Edmond, with an *o.*

Ella remained in New York with James, Jr., and baby Edmund, not yet eighteen months old, while their father traveled, mailing home drafts for money in huge quantities. James O'Neill wrote sadly of his loneliness on the road. When little Edmund was in his second year, his father persuaded Ella to leave seven-year-old Jamie and the baby in the charge of her

O'Neill's Hamlet, one of his fine Shakespearean roles, eclipsed by the popularity of Monte Cristo

mother in their flat in the Richfield on West 43d Street. Reluctantly, Ella agreed.

The O'Neills had brought the *Cristo* troupe into Denver when a letter arrived saying that Jamie had the measles, and had gone into the baby's room, giving him the disease. While Ella was packing, a telegram arrived saying that Edmund had died.

That night, his grieving wife on the New York-bound train, James went onstage as Edmond Dantès. Next day, one review was accompanied by the following article:

AN ACTOR'S SAD BEREAVEMENT

The glitter of the stage display and the glamor which is thrown around the life of a successful actor are all that the audience sees. . . . It knows nothing of the drudgery of an actor's life, nor the anguish which wrings the heart, though the actor seems to be free from care. . . . The inexorable demands . . . were never more painfully exemplified than at last night's performance of *Monte Cristo*. The vast audience did not know that poor Jim O'Neill, who lived as Monte Cristo, was heartbroken. It did not know that at that moment his little child lay dead in far distant New York, and that the agonized mother had just taken a tearful farewell of him to attend the burial of the dear little one. It laughed and clapped its hands and gave no thought but to the actor's genius and dreamed not of the inward weeping that was drowning his heart. But actors are actors and they must strut upon the stage though their hearts break. God pity them; their lot is a hard one.

Ella blamed herself for leaving her children, her husband for requiring her presence, and her son for giving measles to the baby. She whisked Jamie off to Notre Dame Academy at Notre Dame, Indiana, not far from the St. Mary's Academy of her youth.

As for James O'Neill, he lost himself in work. In a bold stroke, he bought the *Monte Cristo* script from owner John Stetson. Costumes, props, and scenery and all went with the deal—even the precious canvas waves became his alone.

"The play is squeezed dry," Stetson told him.

"We shall see," said O'Neill.

Monte Cristo drew as never before.

What was it, this play that could sweep a nation? There have been similar phenomena: *Uncle Tom's Cabin* stayed on the road for years; Joseph Jefferson was to play *Rip Van Winkle* intermittently for forty years.

O'Neill was to play Dantès more than six thousand times, sprinkled and seasoned with Hamlets and Virginiuses and other roles. *Tom* struck at injustice. *Rip* triumphed over death, and got even with his nagging wife. Both, like *Monte Cristo,* were rousing shows, great excitement or fun. *Cristo* was something more. In the story, a poor man, wrongly accused, suffers interminably, avenges himself, and gains untold wealth and high social status. This was a play that exalted and rewarded the common man. Everywhere it toured, people turned out who had been strangers to the theater.

For O'Neill, it embodied his life story—rags to riches through suffering. How the money rolled in—the treasure of Monte Cristo!

O'Neill bought a permanent summer place where the family could be together. Ella's mother had moved to New London, Connecticut, to be with a sister, and James, visiting, grew enthusiastic about this pretty city on the Thames River, with its steady traffic in sailing ships and surrounding dairy country.

James O'Neill had become, to put it bluntly, a road man. Each summer, puttering with the hedges and lawns of his New London estate, he refurbished his self-image. Each fall he headed for the circuit and *Monte Cristo*. The money rolled in. This was "Monte Cristo Cottage": well made, snug, and ample. With his and his wife's money, he dabbled in real estate, bought stock in businesses and in distant gold mines. Any promoter with an Irish name could sell him.

Reporters came out from smaller Connecticut papers to interview the celebrity. He filled them with stories. But seasoned critics who remembered his great promise, the promise of another Booth, were much displeased, and scornful:

"In [James O'Neill's] hands [*Monte Cristo*] has degenerated into an extravagant melodrama. The romance that amused and interested the intellectual world has become a bit of coarse theatricalism, that pleases only the more ignorant of theatre-goers. . . . He is reaping the pecuniary profit of his business sagacity, but it is at the cost of art. If the actor concerned had no previous claim upon critical consideration the matter would not deserve so much comment, but James O'Neill has done admirable work—artistic work—in the past, and it is a cause of regret that he should have abandoned his better abilities."

There was something slick and exciting about the O'Neill business operation, however. Playing several of the character roles in disguise to reduce costs, James moved from city to town with a compact group.

Road companies were relatively new. In the days of Forrest and Junius Booth, the stars toured alone and were backed up by local repertory companies with whom they were often mismatched.

With the rapid spread of railroads, the opportunity arose for relatively luxurious dining and sleeping cars for actors and actresses. The first to jump at the chance was Dion Boucicault, an enterprising Irish actor-manager-playwright who for thirty years had supplied the American stage with slick adaptations lifted from novels.

To protect his plays, Boucicault lobbied hotly for U.S. copyright law, and got the legislation passed—meanwhile stealing from European writers.

One of Boucicault's most original and successful pieces was *The Octoroon; or, Life in Louisiana,* dealing with a bankrupt planter's love for the illegitimate daughter of his father's brother. The girl is finally brought to the auction block, for her mother had been a slave. In a trick ending, Boucicault exposed a murderer whose picture had been taken by a self-tripping camera.

In *The Octoroon,* Boucicault presented Louisa Lane Drew, who held it in her repertory for many years. With her husband, fashionable actor John Drew, a gentleman's gentleman, she toured in company in Boucicault's successful *Colleen Bawn.* After a New York smash, Boucicault considered taking the play to Europe, then hit on his novel railroad scheme.

As the years went down, more touring troupes appeared, and their special cars were a common sight on the railroads. The life gained in luxury and permanence for O'Neill, and then as competition mounted and the profit from *Cristo* declined somewhat, he resolved to change his lot, to produce serious plays, Shakespeare, and other art. Besides, Ella expected another child, and would want him near her in New York. In New York fine things could be done for sensible audiences.

James O'Neill was forty-two. He had reached an age when men question the value of their work. Word reached him of the decline in health of Edwin Booth, whose encouraging words he remembered so well; was there still time?

The year was 1888. On October 16, the O'Neills' third male child was born, and they named him Eugene Gladstone. From the windows of the Barrett House on 43d Street, as they held him, they could see Broadway; to its glory this son would contribute more than Booth and James O'Neill together.

8

The Son of Monte Cristo

ONE OF THE EARLIEST PICTURES of Eugene O'Neill—he is about six—shows a boy sitting on a rock by the sea, at New London, Connecticut, gazing placidly over the water. His happiest times were those New London summers, where he was *home* at the family's Monte Cristo Cottage, on the estuary of the Thames River. There he had a room that was not in a hotel.

From the start, life had been move, move, move. James O'Neill, inspired by the birth of his son, had attempted a new role, starring in *The Envoy,* by Swartz, at the Star Theatre, in New York. If the play should succeed, he planned to finance a succession of important New York productions, in order to stabilize Ella's life with Eugene. The play failed.

James O'Neill told reporters: "New York is the town of towns for fads, skits and horseplay. The dramatic outlook is black. Perhaps, though, it is not the people, but the financial state of the country that is to blame. It is my experience that when the country is going through bad times . . . the people . . . want to see light plays that do not tax the brain."

Under that blanket alibi James O'Neill, Ella, little Gene, and a lusty nurse named Sarah Sandy took to the road with good old reliable *Count of Monte Cristo.* This, James considered a "light play."

Eugene's first memories of his mother involved her fears for his health. "You were born afraid because I was so afraid to bring you into the world," his fictional mother was to tell him in the play *Long Day's Journey Into Night,* ". . . afraid all the time I carried you. I knew something terrible would happen."

In the play he named himself Edmund, after his dead brother, who had died as a baby and become a family ghost, trotted out when it suited Ella's mood. Often she withdrew completely, aided by patent medicines containing morphine, to which she became steadily more addicted.

O'Neill at eleven, on the veranda of Monte Cristo Cottage, with his father and brother

Ella Quinlan O'Neill, Eugene's mother, model for the tragic Mary Tyrone in *Long Day's Journey Into Night*

Little Gene often found her in a trance. Sometimes she lay abed, rocking a large doll, calling to her dead child. Wandering the house abstracted, her eyes dilated, she ignored her small son, mystifying and hurting him.

James O'Neill had discovered her addiction early—when he helpfully insisted on going himself to have her prescription refilled.

"What is this stuff?" he asked the druggist.

"Morphine," came the flat answer, for its dangers were then not fully known.

"My wife started using it to relieve the pains which followed the birth of our son," explained O'Neill. "She uses more and more. She grows distraught when the supply runs out."

O'Neill could not help realizing that his wife, no longer in pain, sought a twilight zone in which to escape her fears. It was not inherent in his intense, self-perfecting personality to try to change, to become a more accommodating husband.

On the one hand, James saw to it that while traveling with Ella, Eugene was provided with an excellent nurse, Sarah Sandy, who took him to parks and zoos and museums. On the other, he failed to encourage Ella in her music and instead, ridiculed her when she lamented her lost chance. Monte Cristo, however, could weep over failure to become the greatest Shakespearean actor since Booth.

Early in childhood, these tensions magnified Gene's animosity toward his father, whom he watched all too often emerge from the canvas waves, heroic and unreal, dripping with sparkling salt, to proclaim that the world was his.

Veneered with heroism and self-confidence, James was rendered all the more vulnerable to the child's inherent perspicacity. Gene revealed his opinion of his father's acting one summer.

James had ordered the manufacture of base-metal statuettes of the Count of Monte Cristo, thinly gold-plated, for sale at theaters and stores. A box of these was kept at the summer estate. One day he went to get one for a friend. Opening the box he found that someone had ruined the glittering figurines by drenching them in a cascade of ugly green enamel.

Some cause for both Ella's and Gene's tendency to withdrawal could be observed by the shrewder of the many men James O'Neill invited to the house, in an endless chain of conviviality and pontification. O'Neill had become a professional bore, an institution, an oracle.

His fans called him silver-tongued, the most beautiful voice on the stage. That voice heard interminably in private proved hard to listen to.

Eugene would hunch up somewhere reading. A friend said, "It's no fun to play at his house. He's always got his nose in a book." What better way to escape the Count of Monte Cristo?

James's influence was not without merit, however. His powers of expression were often original. Self-educated, he drew widely from the classics to express his convictions, often quoting Shakespeare. In fact, Will might as well have lived and traveled with the O'Neills, for what James lacked in successful portrayal of the classics, he made up for in invocations of the Bard.

While some men sing in the tub, James's bathroom rang with the lines of *Hamlet, Midsummer Night's Dream,* and the rest. Scrubbed, dried, talcumed, and smug, admonishing everyone present, he arrived at table the grand old-fashioned father.

Jamie was home from school, gently guiding Gene in the art of father ridicule. "The Count seems a little tight," he might whisper. Shy Gene admired his brother's courage.

Eugene soon became a corner in a terrible square of tensions: an ambitious father, a drug-addicted mother, and a hateful, guilt-ridden elder brother who had been blamed for Edmund's illness.

When he grew older, Jamie told Eugene how he had contracted measles first, had been ordered to keep from the baby's room, and had disobeyed that order. Later, Jamie blamed Eugene for his mother's addiction, because Gene's birth had caused the pain that first made her take morphine.

It would be many years before the urge to write plays dominated Eugene O'Neill. Looking to formative forces, one finds a peculiar circumstance. At the age of seven, Gene was abruptly sent from home, far from his mother, to the Academy of Mount St. Vincent School, at Riverdale, just outside Manhattan.

James O'Neill strode the lovely grounds with his little son in tow, rhapsodizing about its illustrious history. Why, this was the Gothic granite castle which the great Edwin Forrest had built for himself and his wife— and here was the gardener's cottage, where the boys now lived and studied—the very cottage in which Forrest had lived alone.

What an ironic choice of schools, yet how proud this father seemed that he could offer the little man some heritage in consolation for his loneliness!

The parents brought him to school the autumn of 1897, to a new world of iron grille fences, gray stone buildings, and stern women in flowing black robes. Years later, Sister Mary Florentine, who knew Eugene well, remembered that he was most quiet, a constant reader, and that he twitched his head from time to time. However, she noted that when time came for swimming in the Hudson, water seemed to hold a fascination for him. On the Hudson as on the Connecticut river Thames he could watch the steamships and sailing craft as they caught the tide for far-off places. When could he go to the romantic parts of which he had read? What new life could he find beyond this lonely time and the insufficient pages of his books?

For the most part Gene O'Neill brooded and read. His loneliness was so noticeable that when he begged to have his dog sent to live with him, special permission was granted.

This loyal hound was named Perfumery, and many the romp she and Gene had enjoyed upon the banks of the river or the stony beaches of New London, watching the gay ships flying along, gallants and top-gallant sails gleaming in the sun. So the letter was written, a letter of crucial importance; Gene could almost feel the furry weight of his dog nestled at the foot of his bed.

The reply was not rapidly forthcoming, for it brought bad news. Not many weeks before, poor Perfumery had been run down and killed by a carriage.

The intensity of this disappointment is hard to imagine, but it un-questionably drove Gene into the fantasy life where he stayed for some time to come. It was two years before he spoke again to the woman who had been caring for the dog.

Determinedly he sought peace in a world of dreams and in God and his relation to his son, Jesus. These may have become substitutes for his mother and Sarah Sandy, both of whom had deserted him.

Gene's closest friend at boarding school was Joe McCarthy, an or-phaned boy, perhaps because Mr. and Mrs. O'Neill were so often on the road with *Monte Cristo* at holiday time and Gene, like Joe, received no visitors. Long after, he brooded about those years, becoming depressed and quiet as Christmas approached.

Once when grown, he wrote to McCarthy, "Do you ever think of Sister

Martha who used to knuckle us on the bean?" But it was loneliness rather than knuckling which took him into fantasy.

The summers were another scene at Monte Cristo Cottage in New London—swimming, sun, sand, counting the days.

In summer there was time to get to know his great father, who when not Shakespearizing, was philosophizing. A favorite subject was *soul*.

"The man who feels," James said melodiously, "who aspires, who wanders in thought from this world and mingles with the higher intelligences, has a soul that lends itself to artistic effort; in short he is a genius. He may be a poet, a painter or an actor, and I am proud to say that in my profession there have been many geniuses; though alas, they are growing smaller in number by the year, for the sensation monger has supplanted the poet, and the sycophant counter jumper has usurped the place of the real actor."

One can see big brother Jamie blowing out his cheeks in suppression of a laugh, for he dared not laugh, and Gene glancing suspiciously at them both, but feeling it true, as Jamie insisted, that their father was not the great actor, but in fact a ham.

At school again in the fall he felt reassured. Many fellow students respected him as the son of Monte Cristo, and when they dodged the nuns long enough to cut swords from saplings, to duel to the fabled and lethal count of "One—two—*three!*" they wondered why the slender fellow with the penetrating brown eyes did not join them.

Gene graduated from primary school and stood on the edge of change from boyhood to manhood.

For the first time in many years, the O'Neills spent Christmas together, and a happier time it seemed, with James O'Neill about to launch another production of Monte Cristo, the likes of which the world had never seen —why, it would knock all the motion pictures into a cocked hat. Jamie was there. He was now a traveling salesman for a lumber company, but he was talking about acting in the new play. And Gene was there, happy in the fall term of De La Salle, a school in Manhattan that let him live at home where his mother was.

James O'Neill's latest lunge toward public acclaim revealed his insecurity about money. On the one hand, he pursued the classics, discussing cultural acting ventures with any producer who would listen. On the other, he struggled to maintain and improve a standard of living befitting his reputation. To do this he must muster ways not only to battle vaudeville, but the inroads of motion pictures into theater box office receipts as well. This was 1900. Edison's portable Kinetograph was producing one-reelers as part of regular vaudeville bills. Although schoolboys couldn't often join adults at these thrilling spectacles, they slipped downtown— Gene often with the help of Jamie—spending their nickels in Edison Kinetoscope machines to peep at flickering playlets. At table, Gene's enthusiasm keenly reminded his father of the success of these inventions.

"Insidious," said James O'Neill. "A single troupe of actors makes a single film, and this by technical methods is duplicated into the thousands and spread like the plague from coast to coast. We serious actors will soon starve."

To rub salt in his wounds, R. G. Hoffman's film presentation of James's beloved *Passion* play was shown at the Eden Music Theatre in New York, starring no one named O'Neill.

The great producer A. J. Liebler assured James O'Neill that a spectacular production of *Monte Cristo* could draw against vaudeville and films, but no expense should be spared; this posed a financial venture beyond O'Neill's means. Liebler was true to his word regarding expense. Stage hands faced Herculean tasks in this production: a full-rigged ship was towed across the stage; a candelabra 36 feet tall was flown overhead; in one scene a prison of frightening dimensions crowded the actors; forests and villages appeared and disappeared. Audiences of a simple sort should love this spectacle. They did.

James opened in Boston, went on tour.

Gene continued in school, doing well. One afternoon he returned to the apartment, entering in his quiet way, and caught his mother injecting morphine.

With this sudden confrontation, he at last understood his mother's problem. He realized her periodic vacations had been to sanitariums. In reaction he turned to God. He would do anything, he promised in his prayers, if God would cure her.

Week after week Ella O'Neill's wide eyes and distracted manner indicated a prolonged binge. Gene faced this trial alone. There was little that aging nurse Sarah Sandy could do to comfort him, and his father was altogether occupied in his great *Monte Cristo* production. Soon Jamie joined his father to fill the role of Edmond Dantès' son.

With Ella's new lapse, James's first move had been to place Gene with the De La Salle boarding students, where life was rather Spartan. Classmates remembered him as "a dreamy youngster, generally lost in himself . . . polite but taciturn and withdrawn . . . not interested in sports or any of the school activities but always reading . . . no youthful outbursts."

O'Neill became friendly with only one boy, Victor Ridder, a cripple. "I was lame and he was quiet," Ridder said years after. "We were pushed around by the livelier boys. De La Salle was great for sports—football, baseball, floor hockey—but Eugene never showed interest in any of them."

Another friend was Ricardo Amazaga, a Cuban of real warmth, who recalled: "I liked him the first time we met. . . . We both were studious and well-behaved. . . . One time he took a few of us to see *Monte Cristo* —we had a box—and afterward backstage to meet his father, who was friendly and very gracious. . . . In later years when he became famous and I read about the kind of plays he wrote, about his going to sea and bumming around, I thought it must be another O'Neill. . . . It saddens me to think that O'Neill went through so much physical and moral suffering in his path through life."

Eugene finished this year in good form, taking sixth place in a class of twenty-two, with an 88 in history, and an 87 in English, though his marks in mathematics were and would continue to be very low. During the year, he had attended Mass with eagerness; his religion grade for the year stood at 84. He retained his faith.

That summer at New London, although maintaining the habit of church attendance, he insisted that if he must go to boarding school, it should be nonsectarian. His father relented, selecting Betts Academy of Stamford, Connecticut.

It was in this small secluded haven overlooking Long Island Sound from Strawberry Hill that Gene first read the jarring lines of unconventional writers already breaking new ground on the stages of Europe.

If Gene, after seven years at a Catholic school, expected the routine at Betts to be easy, he was wrong. While headmaster "Billy" Betts was more sound than fury, he did hold to the motto, "What we do, we do well." Gene was pitched headlong into the world of mathematics.

Algie Walter took him on, remembering in later years that "he hated math. I got him past algebra into geometry but could never get him into trigonometry. He was stubborn. He had a very determined mind of his own."

As the situation at home worsened, Gene intensified his battle with authority.

His first summer away from Betts was spent at New London. The season began with constant fog and rain, making travel extremely difficult. Blockaded by the weather, Ella exhausted her supply of morphine, and one night, driven mad by the tortures of withdrawal, she ran to the river to throw herself in. Her sons and husband followed. At water's edge they grappled with her as she screamed.

Many years later, in *Long Day's Journey Into Night,* O'Neill said, "Papa and Jamie decided they couldn't hide it from me any more. Jamie told me. I called him a liar! I tried to punch him in the nose. But I knew he wasn't lying. God, it made everything in life seem rotten!"

Next day the couple took council. They could not stay at New London; they would go to the Adirondacks, Ella to a sanitarium. Jamie joined a stock company in Massachusetts. So the summer passed.

It was another boy who returned to Betts. "He would never become actively angry," a friend recalled, "but would withdraw into himself and sulk. In fact he generally seemed lost in himself." Teachers had to prod: "Wake up, O'Neill." A friend recalled that O'Neill did not say much, "but when he did he used fine English and seemed to weigh every word. It took him a long time to get something out."

O'Neill authority Louis Sheaffer has suggested that "this slow, ruminative manner marked him all his life, and indeed, developed to such an extreme degree that people would cut in on him, thinking he had finished, as he lingered among his thoughts and groped for words."

However, certain subjects released from O'Neill, even at Betts in his sixteenth year, a veritable torrent of words. One such subject was the sea, for the work of Jack London captivated him. Another subject on which he expressed himself rather eloquently was illegitimacy. With rigid conviction, Gene stunned his friends by saying that certain advantages went with bastardy, for then you were not annoyed with the troubles of a family. The notion is a pretty straightforward indication that he found the complexities of life with his mother too difficult.

Ingrown though he was, Gene had ways to blow off steam, often ingenious ways.

One night he led a group that built a pyramid of chamber pots at the head of the dormitory stairs. Late, when all the teachers were asleep, the gentle tug of a rope sent the heavy porcelain vessels thundering downward.

Sometimes, after midnight, the soft thudding of feet on the roof meant that Gene O'Neill was pacing under the stars, enjoying a forbidden smoke.

Some nights the boys tied sheets together, slithering to the ground for the half-mile run to the center of Stamford. The attractions included local girls, a horse-drawn dinner wagon that served hamburgers, and a tavern operated by world heavyweight champion Bob Fitzsimmons, not one to raise the sawdust when the bartender slipped a beer to the young fugitives.

It was here, as well as on the docks of New London and at the farmhouses of Connecticut tenant farmers, that O'Neill developed his love of the colorful vernacular of everyday people whose plight so moved him.

O'Neill sat at the feet of the great Fitzsimmons, listening to tales of his boxing exploits. Fitzsimmons was then fully forty years of age and had, the previous July, suffered his second defeat at the hands of Jim Jeffries, but he impressed on the boy his determination to recapture his crown. Fitzsimmons liked to reminisce about his youth in New Zealand and Australia. But nothing could affect O'Neill more than that fierce ambition. The sixteen-year-old boy who had been so emotionally battered could walk the long night mile back to school shivering with inspiration. You could win; you could fight through. It was a hard climb up slippery, dew-soaked sheets, like as not to find a waiting note from headmaster Betts—yet all well worth it.

Next morning, Gene would settle happily with his books, content at having lost a weekend pass home. Years later a friend would remember, "He dreaded the passing of each day because it brought him closer to the end of the school term." With school's end he must face the uncertainties of family life.

In 1923, O'Neill was to write to Betts: "I was tickled to death to get your letter and also an old Betts book. The photos in the latter made me feel quite aged, and a bit melancholy . . . but it wasn't an unpleasant sadness. My memories of Betts are all delightful ones."

With graduation from Betts, his defenses against the shock of his mother's addiction and attempted suicide vanished. As the lines of a later play would prove, "He abased and humbled himself before the Cross," then saw that no miracle would happen. Something snapped in him finally. "He cursed his God and denied Him, and, in revenge, promised his soul to the Devil—on his knees, when everyone thought he was praying."

Rebellious and forlorn, Gene joined Jamie in jaunts to New York where the objective was beer and stronger drink, and eventually a tumble with whatever girls came easily.

Jamie's irresponsibility had become his trademark. He tried acting, and when touring with his father, did whatever he could to embarrass and defeat him. In a scene where James knelt, Jamie tore a strip of muslin with his hands, as though his father's tights had split. It brought down the house.

The older brother liked to keep separate quarters, where he drank and was entertained by prostitutes, who often flocked to the theater to sit, rouged and grinning, in a special box provided by the thoughtful Jamie.

James O'Neill was not without patience—he drank himself. Too, he saw in Jamie his only hope for a theatrical heir, placing some confidence in the boy's better education, wishing that he might become the Shakespearean his father had not. So he put up with an insufferable amount of disobedience.

Jamie liked to taunt. He introduced shocking *double-entendres* into plays, sending up a howl in the audience. Now and then he actually turned up on stage drunk; on one such occasion his father broke into tears at the sight of him.

Little chance then that shy Eugene might join his father and brother in their unhappy occupation. Once, on a bet, he memorized a long dissertation. "You certainly have a good memory," his father said, "but never go on the stage."

Critics were not kind to Jamie, although when sober he could give a creditable performance. Naturally the older boy sought support from young Gene, and together they soon were touring the bars and brothels of Bradley Street, New London, and Broadway.

Jamie admitted his influence: "I made it awful easy for the Kid to sin," he bragged. Writing in *Strange Interlude,* O'Neill revealed his true feelings about these early encounters with vice. Through the character Charlie Marsden, a puritanical writer, he said, "Always that memory! . . . Prep school . . . Easter vacation . . . that house of cheap vice . . . Jack, the dead game sport. . . . 'Take her!' . . . daring me. . . ."

O'Neill could write this because his experience differed so much from his brother's. Where Jamie considered the best of these women delicious vermin, to Gene they were outcasts like himself—lonely, rejected, and equally troubled. In several early plays he treated their plight with detailed compassion. Whatever his reluctance, however, he was soon drinking and carousing with the worst.

His first summer before college was one of willfulness and wandering. He took nourishment where he found it. The rebelliousness of adolescence is well understood by adults, but seldom has an adolescent understood his own formative forces as thoroughly as did O'Neill.

The shock of two discoveries—his hatred of his father, and his mother's addiction, caused by the pain of his own birth—may well have started his drinking.

When the autumn of 1906 rolled around, Eugene O'Neill, tall, lanky, and handsome in a solemn way, drank a final whisky with brother Jamie, and entered Princeton University, his large eyes burning soulfully beneath the rim of a freshman beanie.

9
Rebellion

EUGENE ACKNOWLEDGED his acceptance at Princeton as though it were a challenging glove slap across his face. His response to that challenge of new authority was ribald good humor, self-destruction, and animosity toward his father.

He had been placed in a clearly understood position. Whereas 25 percent of Princeton students worked to help support their studies, Eugene was not required to lift a finger. Though he had always accused his father of tightness, he received ample spending money, so that with tuition his expenses for the first—and last—nine months totaled $1,400. It was an arrangement indicating that he must perform. Well, he had performed at Mount St. Vincent, De La Salle, and Betts, and that might be enough.

Gene was quartered in the upper floor of University Hall, a musty old building that he did his best to enliven. He decorated his room with theatrical souvenirs, posters, playbills, brassieres, stockings, and slippers. He burned incense. Above him glowed an electric bulb in a red shade, as he perused the poets and philosophers, cigarette dangling from his lips, at his elbow a glass of absinthe.

His fellows found him admirably odd.

He sallied forth, usually utterly unprepared for spherical trigonometry, an exquisite torture to his distracted brain. One can see him passing slowly under the stately elms before Nassau Hall, the administration building, late for class; college president Woodrow Wilson behind a large window may have gazed with brief disapproval upon this nonconformist—for Wilson was in the midst of a campaign to turn the student body away from sports and other nonacademic diversions. This boy certainly seemed diverted.

Some classmates liked this scowling "black Irishman," this well-dressed Broadway *bon vivant,* who was so much better read than anyone in his class. Sipping his absinthe and burning incense, he recited poetry; he would become a poet—having been brought up in the theater, he said, he could see through its superficiality.

Many of the boys had seen *Monte Cristo*; it was a great show. Forget it, said Gene, for it was bad stuff. However, "The Old Man" was all right, he admitted, letting his meaning come through with his hesitation.

Gene's friends noticed that when he lacked drink he often brooded; drunk or not, he never laughed, though his smile could be infectious.

O'Neill did well in English and history; by midterm he held a passing average in all his courses. So he relaxed and accelerated his recreation.

As he had let his brother, Jamie, influence him, he now found in an older friend, Louis Holliday, an inspiration to break more chains. Holliday was big, sandy-haired, deceptively well-mannered. (He would one day die of an overdose of heroin.) Eagerly this radical and free-thinker introduced Gene to Manhattan's burgeoning Bohemia, whose limits far exceeded those of the theater world. Perched flatteringly on the fringe, O'Neill absorbed heady philosophies.

Gene took root in these radical byways, where Bernard Shaw's social-ism was well aired and each new translation of Nietzsche sold out rap-idly. The focus of New York's intellectual activity was Benjamin R. Tucker, owner of the Unique Book Shop at 30th Street and Sixth Ave-nue, which contained "the largest collection of advanced literature in the world."

Holliday could tout Gene to Tucker for the extent of his reading. Tucker may have let Gene know, in time, that he himself had read well at the age of two, and at four had discovered that the Episcopal Prayer Book had misquoted Scripture. Then in his fifties, a mild businessman in appearance, he was nevertheless one of America's leading radicals, "an individual anarchist," resolute and effective. His magazine *Liberty* had been the first to publish Shaw in America. Tucker reminded Gene, when the latter's grades plummeted in the spring of his freshman year, that Shaw had calmly turned his back on higher education.

O'Neill preferred to let the Princeton administration evict him. Holli-day, despite his sophistication, joined O'Neill in typical, naïve collegiate escapades, which did not add to his favor with the dean. One drinking orgy led to O'Neill's characteristic release of hostility; raging, he smashed his room furniture, tore out bureau drawers. When his revolver tumbled to the floor, he seized it, aimed it at Holliday, and pulled the trigger again and again. The gun was empty.

Louis Holliday laughed with wild relief. Good old Gene.

Warned on grades, O'Neill frolicked. "I have not loved the world," he would quote Byron, "nor the world me; I have not flatter'd its rank breath, nor bowed to its idolatries a patient knee."

Weekend escapades took him to New York or Trenton. In Manhattan, he might stop at the Lucerne to "put the bite on the Old Man," after explaining the need for fresh money and assuring James that all went well academically.

In Trenton, Gene consorted with prostitutes even Holliday could not stomach. He had seen Ibsen's *Hedda Gabler* in that spring of 1907 and seized on its suggestion that the immoral act might be the right and kind act.

He began to devour Shaw's "The Quintessence of Ibsenism"; the forces were building toward social realism, with relentless concern for the individual. The quintessence of Shavianism, Eugene found to be concern with social ideas as embodied in the lives of his characters. Having discovered *Mrs. Warren's Profession* in script at Tucker's, O'Neill wondered at the success of this London play—first refused license— which openly discussed organized prostitution. (Mrs. Warren's daughter learns that her mother had graduated from the profession to operate a chain of brothels throughout Europe.)

However, Shaw's ideologically humorous style confused Gene; he had faced in himself and others too many terrible truths to veer far from tragedy. Shaw had not suffered, except from a similar shyness. O'Neill was more permanently affected by Nietzsche, whose *Thus Spake Zarathustra,* newly translated into English, affirmed his individuality, rebelliousness, and agnosticism.

Nietzsche concerned himself only with the individual. "How can one praise and glorify a nation as a whole?—even among the Greeks, it was the individuals that counted," O'Neill would read. "The Greeks are interesting and extremely important because they reared such a vast number of great individuals. How was this possible?"

How, O'Neill wondered, might he become a great individual? In Nietzsche he found comfort that he might continue doing as he pleased: "It is the same with man as with the tree. The more he seeketh to rise unto the height and light, the more vigorously do his roots struggle earthward, downward, into the dark and deep—into the evil."

O'Neill joined Holliday in New York that spring to report his dismissal at Princeton and a terrible blowout with his father, who had pointed out that, like Jamie, Gene had botched his best chance at a decent education—"Something I never had."

All his life, O'Neill would point to Nietzsche as his most profound influence. "But the worst enemy thou canst meet," he would quote to Holliday, "wilt thou thyself always be; thou waylayest thyself in caverns and forests. Thou lonesome one, thou goest the way to thyself!"

So he did.

He found love where he could, on a short and disciplinary allowance. Strolling the summer streets, he comforted himself by interviewing the prostitutes who disported themselves at the Haymarket, once known as Satan's Circus, a labyrinth of gambling rooms, bars, and bedrooms. Sympathetic and genuinely tuned to their suffering, he made his way. His companions were usually Holliday, Edward Keefe, and George Bellows. Bellows founded the Ash Can School of painting, and like O'Neill, saw beauty in the ugliness around them.

Mornings, Gene fought sleep trying to compose his impressions in poems:

> In sleek dress suit an old man sits and leers
> With vulture mouth and blood-shot, beady eyes
> At the young girl beside him. Drunken tears
> Fall down her painted face, and choking sighs
> Shake her, as into his familiar ears
> She sobs her sad, sad history—and lies!

Were they Gene's ears? Listen as he might, Eugene could not convert his emotion into effective verse. The great French poet Paul Valéry said, "The writer consumes everything he is and everything around him. His pleasures and griefs, his business, his God, his childhood, his wife, his friends and enemies, his knowledge and ignorance—all are tossed onto the fateful paper. Some there are who bring on a crisis, irritate a wound, or cherish their sufferings so as to write of them, and since the invention of 'sincerity' as valid literary currency . . . there is no fault, anomaly, or reserve which has not acquired its value."

It seemed as though Gene in his rebellion would exert his life toward this judgment while his roots struggled earthward.

Though his poetry lacked originality, he did work hard at it. In the winter of 1909 he took Keefe and Bellows to a run-down farm his father owned at Zion, New Jersey. While his friends painted in the freezing shack, O'Neill fed the stove and wrote sonnets.

From time to time, he attended New York plays. *The Truth,* a comedy of manners by Clyde Fitch, the first American to attract international attention, was one of a large number of dramas which that author laid at the doorstep of the new realism. O'Neill saw through it: superficial detail substituted for what he knew to be the grit of life.

In Edward Sheldon's vividly realistic work, *Salvation Nell,* Gene found another stone for his dramatic philosophy. A remarkable young playwright, Sheldon seized on true detail to expose the inner self and its relation to the world. *Theatre Magazine* called it a triumph of stage management and acting, pointing out that many things in a play did not depend on the written word.

In one scene, the scrubwoman heroine held her drunken lover's head in her lap for fully ten minutes without a word. This would return to O'Neill's mind as he saw again and again in the lower depths scenes of pathos that fell beyond articulate expression.

Realism and naturalism never overwhelmed the otherwise impressionable wanderer. He saw nothing new in the "new realism." In ancient Greece, the tragedian Theodoros had been praised for a delivery extremely natural, and for using his voice not like an actor's but like that of an ordinary person.

At that time, Gene had no interest in the classic drama. Shakespeare left him cold. So he was somewhat amused when the elder O'Neill returned to town in a fit of optimism to rehearse *Julius Caesar,* in one of his last attempts at respectability.

Having been forced to take a job—in a cheap jewelry firm James owned—Gene retaliated by laughing at the aging Caesar. More amusing was brother Jamie, his hair plastered down in a poor imitation of a Roman.

One New York paper wondered, "Do long runs weaken the player's brain?" (Pictures of Monte Cristo in full regalia.) When *Caesar* failed, a reviewer quipped about James's next play: "The only excitement aroused by his tour in *Honor of the Humble* . . . was the conflagration which mercifully destroyed the scenery."

At this time, Gene O'Neill's courtship of Kathleen Pitt-Smith, a "good girl" he had met at a party, seemed part of his attack on the establishment and his father. Tall, brown-haired, with large blue eyes and a poignant manner, Kathleen fell under the spell of his ardent poetry—and his sensitive expression. Most flattering was his obvious need of comfort. She listened with resolute politeness when his stories of suffering became polemic, drifting into the philosophy of Nietzsche and Schopenhauer. She was in love, blind to his instability. For his part, Gene reserved spectacles of misogynist rage for other women. Together, they drifted into romance. But when Kathleen told him she was pregnant, Gene rushed to his father, who quickly arranged for him to join a mining engineer, Fred C. Stevens, who was leaving soon on a gold prospecting expedition in Spanish Honduras.

Though Gene may have loved Kathleen, the prospect of marriage and its responsibility frightened him. James was adamant in his view that considering Gene's inability to support a wife, and Kathleen's being Protestant, marriage was out of the question; he remained in ignorance of the pregnancy. Gene agreed to work with Stevens. However, he secretly married Kathleen at Trinity Protestant Episcopal Church in Hoboken, New Jersey, on October 2, 1909.

Soon after, young O'Neill set off by railroad to join Stevens on the West Coast. To see him off at Grand Central were his father and Kathleen. She found Mr. O'Neill very gracious and pleasant.

This escapade had an easy attraction for Gene O'Neill. In the new century, America looked to the Latin lands—what better goal than treasure? And for a time, there would be an end to his father's insistence that he return to school. The escape took O'Neill for the first time to sea. His delight in the free and open expanse of the Pacific was short-lived; soon he exchanged that view for "the forest . . . wall of darkness dividing the world," as he would put it in *The Emperor Jones*. "Only when the eye becomes accustomed to the gloom can the outlines of separate trunks of the nearest trees be made out, enormous pillars of deeper blackness. A somber monotone of wind lost in the leaves moans in the air. Yet this sound serves but to intensify the impression of the forest's relentless immobility."

But at sea or in the jungle he could not escape from the guilt of knowing that soon, in America, his child would be born. Finally, wracked by malaria, he returned to a coastal port, where a U.S. consul, short of blankets, wrapped him in some spare flags for the night. "I looked just like George M. Cohan," he wrote his parents, thinking of Cohan's role in *Yankee Doodle Dandy*. His spirit apparently undimmed, he headed home. At the Hotel Lucerne, he found the apartment empty, threw his bags down, and got himself a drink. Unpacking while he drank, he found his scarred machete. Unsheathing it, he swung the blade. Around him he saw the confining accouterments of respectability, the trappings of his father's success.

When his mother returned, she found him asleep on the floor. The furniture had been hacked to pieces.

Days went by, but Kathleen received no visitor.

Her mother telephoned the newspapers. Next day, the New York *World* carried the following headline: "The Birth of a Boy Reveals Marriage of 'Gene' O'Neill. Young Man in Honduras Doesn't Know He Is Dad. May Not Hear News for Weeks. Working at Mine to Win Fortune for Family."

When Gene appeared at his old haunts, the headlines stated: "Gene O'Neill Home, but Not with Wife."

James O'Neill's reaction to the truth was to hustle his son off with the road company doing *The White Sister,* in the made-work title of assistant company manager. By day, while it played in Boston, he spent his time on Mystic Wharf, talking to the sailors, intrigued by their salty tales and their acceptance of him. He had read all of Conrad and London. What lay beyond these docks? He had had a taste of escape; why not sail farther? Legend would lay his shipping aboard the bark *Charles Racine* to poetic wanderlust. However, a letter exists, dated June 7, 1910, from Capt. Gustav Waage to his employer stating that "the passengers are two boys whom I have been asked to take care of." The Count was again exporting the troublemaker. Gene, bound for Argentina, would for some time fail to feed the gossip columnists.

James O'Neill must have given a lusty wave from dockside and a sad shake of his graying head too. Shortly before, his company had celebrated his sixtieth birthday. He told reporters, "All my years on the stage form one grand poem of happiness to myself."

Looking back, Eugene O'Neill would recount, "I can remember in my

sailor days, what a thrill of release it gave me to feel the great ocean
ground swell start to heave the ship under me. It meant freedom then—
an end to an old episode and the birth of another—for life then was
merely a series of episodes flickering across my mind."

The Boston waterfront had receded; the number of gulls, like tangible
proofs of the land gone, diminished above the wake of the *Charles Racine*.
Gene could imagine his father turning from the wharf with a shrug.

Aboard ship, Gene fell in with the crew. His companion was probably
Louis Holliday, though the record is not clear. The men were an odd lot,
from many parts of the world. He would find them better than men of his
kind, more loyal and generous. "I hate life ruled by conventions," he
admitted in the forecastle during the long smokes. "Your lives have tra-
ditions and conventions, but they are the sort that appeal to me."

Cut off from liquor, O'Neill pitched in to work and thrived.

In a late fine play, he would write, "I lay on the bowsprit facing astern,
with the water foaming into spume under me, the masts with every sail
white in the moonlight, towering high above me. I became drunk with the
beauty and singing rhythm of it, and for a moment I lost myself—actually
lost my life. I was set free! I dissolved in the sea, became white sails and
flying spray, became beauty and rhythm, became moonlight and the ship
and the high dim-starred sky! I belonged, without past or future, within
peace and unity and a wild joy, within something greater than my own
life, or the life of Man, to Life itself! And at such times I was in love with
death."

In his bunk during that first true ocean voyage, he scrawled away at
the poetry which he hoped would make him known:

Weary am I of the tumult, sick of the staring crowd,
Pining for wild sea places, where the soul may think aloud. . . .

I have had my dance with Folly, nor do I shirk the blame;
I have sipped the so-called Wine of Life and paid the price of shame. . . .

Then it's ho! for the plunging deck of a bark, the hoarse song of the crew,
With never a thought of those we left or what we are going to do.

He titled this "Free." With never a thought for Kathleen and the baby
she had named Eugene Gladstone O'Neill, Jr.? Unlikely, callous though
he could be.

O'Neill, like all sailors, spent time sanding the masts, chipping rust—

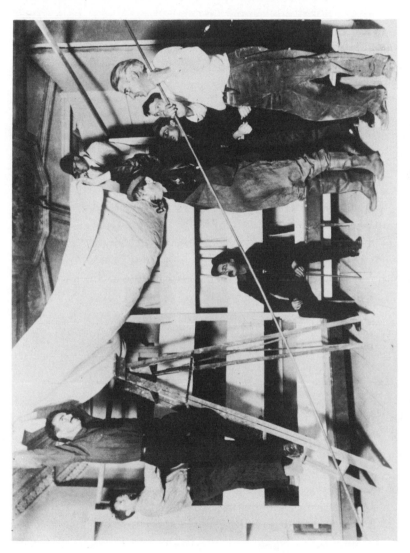

O'Neill, on the stepladder, helps set the scene for *Bound East for Cardiff*, produced by the Provincetown Players, 1916. His experiences at sea were used in writing this early play

the hull was of steel—and singing the various work chanteys such as "Whiskey Johnny" and "Homeward Bound." The food wasn't bad: "something called coffee, and something called tea"; salt pork, fresh bread twice a week, and hardtack served with *plukkfish,* or creamed fish leftovers. Osmunds Christopherson, a crewman, remembered, "O'Neill was well liked on board. We thought him an interesting strange bird we all loved to talk to."

It was a straighter and stronger Eugene O'Neill who walked the gangway to the dock at Buenos Aires, even then a sprawling cosmopolitan city. Settling at the Continental Hotel at $1.70 a day, O'Neill soon doubled with Frederick Hettman, a Stanford University graduate surveyor, in order to conserve funds. Before long, Hettman was being dragged to the hot spots, where Gene told long stories of his father's triumphs and drained his glasses dry. The older man was always first to retire; Gene might turn up next morning, bloody and bleary-eyed, talking of fights and rare delights. The old pattern of self-destruction and pointless excess had been renewed; certainly it seemed true that he was in love with death.

One night in his cups, he told Hettman about Kathleen and their child. "I believe you are sorry for what you have done," Hettman observed. "You have told me the same story two or three times; you really want to get it off your chest."

Inevitably, O'Neill's decline led to sleeping on benches or in the sheet-tin shantytowns near the waterfront, sharing his hovel with a waif of a girl as needful of a home as he.

The southern summer was drawing to a close; from the west the cool wind of the Andes cut across the pampas and made the street sleepers and derelicts of Buenos Aires shiver, Eugene O'Neill among them. He had had, for the time, enough.

Now he found a different punishment; aboard the *Ikala,* bound for New York, as a regular seaman, he joined the rhythm of the industrialized sailors of the age of steam, "hard work, small pay, and bum grub," as he would write in the earliest of his fine plays, "and when we git into port, just a drunk endin' up in a fight, and all your money gone. . . . Never meetin' no nice people; never gittin' outa sailor-town, hardly, in any port; travelin' all over the world and never seein' none of it; without no one to care whether you're alive or dead."

Eugene O'Neill arrived in New York impenitent but curious. He would visit Kathleen. Renting a three-dollar-a-month flop over "Jimmy the

Priest's" bar on Fulton Street, he cleaned up and then summoned his courage for the ordeal.

He was polite. After some small talk, he asked to see the baby. Kathleen later recalled, "He was a beautiful baby. I know all mothers believe that, but I've seen plenty of babies and he really was unusual. His face was all rosy and flushed, the way a baby is when he's been sleeping, and he behaved beautifully when I picked him up. He didn't burst out crying or anything like that, the way most babies will if you suddenly break in on their sleep and hand them to a stranger. He seemed to take to Mr. O'Neill, which pleased me very much. After a while he fell asleep again, in Mr. O'Neill's arms, and I put him back in bed.

"All evening I kept expecting Mr. O'Neill to say why he'd called, why he'd come to see me, but he never did."

O'Neill returned to Jimmy the Priest's, his residence saloon, run by James J. Condon, about fifty, a man of ascetic and religious appearance, whom he was to immortalize as "Johnny the Priest" in the play *Anna Christie*. At Jimmy's he drank and wrote poetry and collected impressions of low life. Often he drank with a tough Liverpool Irishman named Driscoll, a stoker of immense strength who found him congenial.

Desperate again for escape, O'Neill shipped out once more, with Driscoll, on an American Line ship. In the hell of the stokehold he watched the men handling monstrous shovelfuls of coal in fierce heat, as though there on the edge of Hades they searched for and found atonement.

Back again at Jimmy's, in poor health, O'Neill was told that Driscoll was dead, that he had simply jumped overboard.

O'Neill made brief visits to New London in the summer, sometimes leaving behind a poem that the New London *Telegraph* would publish. These efforts were becoming more taut and more than a little honest, as in "Not Understood":

> Not understood. We move along asunder;
> Our paths grow wider as the seasons creep
> Along the years; we marvel and we wonder,
> Why life is life, and then we fall asleep—
> Not understood.

Having deposited this egg to hatch in the nest of Monte Cristo, O'Neill would slip back to his haunts. One day while he was sleeping it off, there was a knock on his door.

There stood an attorney hired by his father. The man announced his good fortune: Kathleen had agreed to a divorce, without alimony or child support. O'Neill seemed bewildered.

Now they required of him evidence of adultery, to satisfy New York State law. Would he cooperate? Would he go with witnesses to a brothel, and there . . . ?

He completed the transaction, then drank himself into an extended binge. He seems to have continued in that fashion until James, ending a tour, arrived in town. Late one evening, Gene visited a series of drugstores, buying a quota of barbiturates at each. He returned to his cheap room, swallowed them all and lay down. But, as his thoughts began to swirl, he changed his mind.

Friends rushed him to Bellevue. When two internes succeeded in reviving him, his buddies taxied to James O'Neill's hotel, asking for $50 to cover the cost of resuscitation.

Told the story, Eugene demanded, "How much do you have left?"

"Thirty-two dollars," was the reply.

"Split!" ordered O'Neill. They drove back to Jimmy's. "I managed to get potted to the gills," he remembered without sadness. "We all thought it was the biggest joke in the whole damn world."

James O'Neill had taken *Monte Cristo* on vaudeville tour; now his son, bedeviled and corrupted by self-hate, pursued him.

Eugene topped a corking drunk by buying a train ticket to New Orleans where *Monte Cristo* was playing. Confronting his father, he agreed to perform minor roles in return for room and board, this with a wink to Jamie. They were off and running.

The details of that western tour are too depressing to detail; the brothers drank their way through performances highlighted by puns, intentional fluffs, and slapstick pranks. Ella operated in the trance of morphine. Audiences showed little interest in the abbreviated Dumas play.

In New York, James faced Eugene desperately. Wouldn't he return to New London and perhaps get a job there reporting for the paper? That could be arranged. Hadn't he had enough?

Eugene O'Neill paid a final visit to Jimmy the Priest's, drank a final drink. "Jimmy," he said, "I'm going home with the Old Man." It may have sounded like quite a switch for the tough guy, but it wasn't. He had won. He had helped beat the Count of Monte Cristo.

10
Consummation

JAMES O'NEILL'S attitude toward his son took a better turn by summer. Gene seemed to be digging in, to be getting organized and getting things done. He seemed to know what he wanted. At the New London *Telegraph,* he wrote the stories that he was asked to write. Why, City Editor Mollan told James himself, "When I bawl out, 'O'Neill!' O'Neill comes to my desk and says, 'Yes, sir.' "

Ella had returned from a sanitarium; she appeared acquiescent.

They seemed headed toward a good summer. Yet the undercurrents, of which O'Neill would write in the autobiographical *Long Day's Journey Into Night,* were seething. Even at this time Gene noted facts and ideas which might find their way into that work of literature, though he would not face the writing of it for thirty years, so painful were the recollections.

In this summer of 1912, hope hung in the balance; the O'Neills were again a family together. Memory of the possibility of their fusion rings throughout the play.

What disrupted their healing—James's ambition again? (*Monte Cristo* reared its head, when a film company offered to make a version.) Jamie's drinking? A lapse on the part of Ella?

All might have gone well had not Eugene contracted tuberculosis. Five months after his return home, he departed for the state sanitarium at Shelton, Connecticut, near New Haven, accompanied by Olive Evans, his nurse. "He was frightened," she would recall, "and said very little. I tried making conversation to get his mind off things but finally had to give up. He just stared out the window most of the time, though I don't imagine he saw what he was looking at. It was snowing when we got off, and three or four coffins were just being transferred from another train to ours. . . . He . . . made some kind of grim joke that that was what was waiting for him at the sanitarium."

Neither James nor his son was impressed with the state facility; he transferred to Gaylord Farm, a sanitarium in Wallingford, Connecticut, where he was judged a mild and very favorable case.

Here he really took stock. Around him men and women faced death without self-pity; he wondered at his own tendency to fault his lot, to seek the bitter way out. Here, too, he had more time to read; among the many books he obtained were the recently translated plays of August Strindberg who, despite an almost pathological hatred of women, did delineate clearly the love-hate balance that shades both normal and abnormal relationships. In Strindberg's *The Dream Play, The Dance of Death,* and *The Father,* O'Neill saw the tortures which members of his own family had inflicted on one another.

In Strindberg, more than in the jovial Shaw or the workmanlike Ibsen, he found a writer who had had the courage to explore with pen the most abysmal parts of his soul. So he placed Strindberg next to Nietzsche in his heart. Like Strindberg, he would become a playwright.

After his discharge, Eugene O'Neill took residence at the Rippins' boarding house, next door to Monte Cristo Cottage. The family had often eaten meals at the Rippins' when Ella was out of sorts. It was a happy, active family providing the perfect backdrop for his self-imposed asceticism.

O'Neill wrote in isolation, in longhand: short plays, one-acters, three about death at sea: *The Web, Fog, Thirst, Warnings, Recklessness.* This spurt proved he could be productive and that he was preoccupied with death—all involved death, some by violence. His father agreed to have them published privately under a single cover, and then bought him a secondhand motor launch. O'Neill sunned himself on its deck daily, in the nude, and took long swims in the frightening, comforting sea, confident that his father, who was busily showing Gene's work around, would succeed in having his plays produced.

In July of 1914 he sent a sampling of his work to George Pierce Baker, professor of play-writing at Harvard, with the message, "I do not think it would be fair to judge me by my Princeton record. I was eighteen then, but now I am fast approaching twenty-six, and the Princeton freshman and I have very little in common. . . . I want to be an artist or nothing." He was accepted.

O'Neill wrote diligently and, in time, wrote well. He submitted plays to film companies and to the new Washington Square Players, who rejected his book of one-acters, and a new play, *Bound East for Cardiff*.

Early in the winter of 1915, he found himself in Greenwich Village in the company of Louis Holliday, who had opened a bar and restaurant called the "Sixty" at 60 Washington Square South. Once again he drifted with the Bohemians, discussing writers and love, drinking. When the Sixty closed, he shifted his patronage to the Golden Swan on Fourth Street, a bar known unofficially as the "Hell Hole." His drinking increased. At the Hell Hole he met Terry Carlin, an aging and insolvent socialist philosopher, widely read and opinionated. Gene had found a foster father.

With spring, Carlin and O'Neill, broke and dispirited, looked for greener pastures. Writers and artists had recently discovered the pleasures and inexpensiveness of Provincetown, an untroubled fishing village amid the sand dunes of Cape Cod. There a group later to become known as the Provincetown Players were to establish an amateur theater using a shack on a wharf. A nice place to spend the summer, O'Neill decided. When he packed his bag, he packed his plays. Terry had a philosophy; it went like this: "If an oyster can turn its pain into a pearl, then, verily, when we have suffered enough, something must arise out of our torture—else the world has no meaning."

The lovely untouched town, the little houses, the sun, the sea, and people who cared about the arts (Jig Cook, who nourished talent in everyone; Susan Glaspell, an excellent writer, and others)—that was Provincetown. O'Neill, though he knew of their plans for a theater, would not approach them. He settled shyly in nearby Truro. One day, Miss Glaspell met Terry, told him of the Provincetown Players' progress, and their lack of a good second bill. "Haven't you a play to read to us?" she asked.

"No," answered Terry. "I don't write, I just think, and sometimes talk. But Mr. O'Neill has got a whole trunk full of plays."

O'Neill was asked to visit Cook's house that evening. *Bound East for Cardiff* was read aloud in the living room while O'Neill skulked in the dining room, afraid of faces. Susan Glaspell recalled, "He was not left alone in the dining room when the reading had been finished. Then we knew what we were for."

Cardiff went into production. This was the first O'Neill play produced.

"The sea has been good to Eugene O'Neill," Glaspell wrote. "It was there for his opening. There was a fog, just as the script demanded. . . . The tide was in, and it washed under us and around, spraying through the holes in the floor, giving us the rhythm and the flavor of the sea while the big dying sailor talked to his friend Drisc of the life he had always wanted deep in the land, where you'd never see a ship."

The wharf shuddered with applause.

Before he left Provincetown, Jig Cook said to a friend, "You don't know his plays, but you will. All the world will know Gene's plays someday. This year, on the night he first came to Provincetown and read us *Bound East for Cardiff,* we knew we had something to go on with. Someday this little theater will be famous; someday the little theater in New York will be famous—this fall the Provincetown Players go to New York with *Cardiff* on their first bill. . . . Gene's plays aren't the plays of Broadway; he's got to have the sort of stage we're going to found in New York."

In the city season in addition to his sea play, O'Neill saw *Before Breakfast* produced, a little horror in which an all but unseen offstage husband, nagged unmercifully by his wife, kills himself behind a closed door. Gene provided an arm, all that was seen of the poor fellow, though he was willing to act and had appeared in *Cardiff.*

This playlet, which did not win reviewers, expressed O'Neill's intense fear of women, payable as hatred. Old James, in town to do a bit part, dropped by to watch rehearsal, and insisted on directing Mary Pyne in the role of the wife.

"Alfred! Alfred! Answer me!" she cried in her closing lines. "What is it you knocked over? Are you still drunk. . . . Alfred!" She stood in the doorway looking down at the floor of the inner room, transfixed with horror.

"My boy," said James charitably when it was over, "why don't you write pleasanter plays?" After changing Miss Pyne's every gesture and inflection, he departed; Gene redirected her. However, father and son had remained calm, their relationship on higher ground.

O'Neill's output increased with its acceptance by little theater. In its verve and flexibility the little theater movement successfully attacked the Broadway establishment, drawing critics and well-heeled playgoers to its folding chairs and drafty halls, much as today's off-Broadway theater does. The critics paid admission.

Eugene O'Neill Hilariously Enters Comic Field

"AH, WILDERNESS," by Eugene O'Neill; Random House. $2.50.

Reviewed by SCULLEY BRADLEY, English Dept., U. of Pa.

IF SOMETIME soon you come upon a friend reading a book and emitting the chuckles and solo guffaws which are universally understood to indicate that a reader is having a very amusing time, you must not conclude that he is reading Mr. Wodehouse or Mrs. Parker.

It is just as likely to be "Ah, Wilderness," the latest play of Eugene O'Neill. Over in New York at the Playhouse of the Theater Guild, where even standing room for "Ah, Wilderness!" was sold out in advance, they are saying they can hardly believe that the author of "Strange Interlude" and "Mourning Becomes Electra" could write a play so comic as this, or a scene so funny as the second act, in which poor "Uncle Sid

drew Aguecheek in "Twelfth Night," in which bibulousness, ribaldry and mirth find their most perfect expression. As a m—— ——t is doubt-ful whether truly great for humorous sion, however In "Ah, Wil "a new O'Ne tain aspects has previou

There is this first c enteenth fu ways, it is t events, or and vivid recollection characters Miller, the the "large cut" (Nev town, of newspaper

O'Neill Hits New Stride in Latest Drama

"Days Without End" Meets Some Adverse Criticism—Analogy Between Shaw and American Dramatist—Local Stage Offerings and Events of Musical Season

A S Bernard Sha———

Richard is central to the plot, what little there is of it. He is having an adolescent "affair" with Mildred, and ——— and sends her verses of Swin-that he could "drink wine, and eat her y," much to the per-r outraged parent, a man who at once est.

really thinks of Mil-adolescent awe and y, is now very much th fortune and men's forbidden to see Mil-ne Fourth of July he speeches (out of Shaw) and goes "out into the middle of the after-g them he will return vborg in "Hedda Gab-: leaves in his hair. or Punishment.

stored to Mildred's favor, although he is condemned to go to Yale for punishment. He is altogether delightful, and the study of his character forms one of the most effective portrayals of the adolescent boy that our stage has witnessed.

Other characters are equally well portrayed. Mr. Nat Miller, the father, is delightful, and one can see why the part tempted George M. Cohan to break his life-long habit of appearing only in plays written by himself. In his hands the part should be among his most memorable accomplishments. And Uncle Sid—well you must read or see the play to appreciate him! When he and Nat come home from the Sachems' picnic that Fourth of July, he is in the sub-liminal stage of squiffiness, and O'Neill has supplied him with lines which should prove immortal.

To see him eat his lobster claws with the shell on is funny, but to ———

'Desire Under the Elms' Upsets All Theories of Producers

O'Neill's Play, With Tragic Doom as a Theme, to Have Run for Thirty-six Weeks on Broadway Makes New Theatrical History

The sight of a play with tragic doom as a theme running thirty-six weeks on Broadway is viewed by the commercial producers with an emotion akin to consternation. Were a hypothetical question covering an abstract case put to any one of them, he would say that it could not be done.

But it has been done, and the end is not yet in sight. The play is Eugene O'Neill's gaunt and granite "Desire Under the Elms," the survivor of at least one terrific set-to with the District Attorney and one minor engagement with the Play Jury. O'Neill's drama is now well past its 300th performance, and its producers are confident that it will prosper until September.

It has long been the theory of the producers who divide their attentions between art and the box office in equal measure that no tragedy could flourish in New York for more than fifteen weeks, and in their arguments they advanced as testimony "Hamlet" and all plays of that general type. To insure a long run and stimulating grosses the play must have a sentimental ending, justice and virtue must emerge triumphant not later than 10:40 and the audience must leave the theater in high good humor.

The experimental theater groups—only the producers call them radical rather than experimental—might tinker with tragedies. It was, in their opinion, more or less the divine prerogative of these dramatists in the embryo to employ tragedy as a gesture. They cited Galsworthy's "Justice," "John Ferguson," St. John Ervine's play which had a truly notable ..n, "The Jest," "Redemption" and ..uiu Vollmer's "Sunup" as instances f exceptional tragedies, expertly quipped and acted, that could not excite a popular response over any such period as 300 performances.

As evidence to support their theory they offered, too, the plays of Eugene O'Neill himself. "The Emperor Jones," "The Hairy Ape," "Beyond the Horizon," not one of these endured for more than twenty weeks. The audience for the tragedy, either native or foreign, is too limited, has been their contention. It is made up of the radi-'ls, the super-sensitive and super-

intelligent. Just as the magazine editors reject the manuscript with a tragic finish, regardless of its merit so, too, ———-

eye its f of r piety "D wich last. sussi playe Stree Thea capac Distr: sire" the O in an nuncii tablisl play arouse Nor since George tion it law. 1 followe attemp produc the pla ments for the ple wit characte Its real deterren Presse produce: Under t and tha estimate. establish a trage statistics lieved th favorably by any tre

"Desire Eugene O writer of this field represente can who is of the Pi his plays in London

New O'Neill Play Hailed in Gotham As Majestic Work

"Mourning Becomes Electra" Has Basis in Grecian Classics

By JOHN MASON BROWN
Public Ledger Bureau
New York, Oct. 31

FOR exciting proof that the theatre is still very much alive, that it still has grandeur and ecstasy to offer to its patrons, that fine acting has not disappeared from behind the footlights' glare, that productions which thrill with memorability are still being made, that scenic design and stage direction can belong among the fine arts and that the Theatre Guild, in spite of any causes for discouragement it may have given in the past, is still the most accomplished as well as the most intrepid producing organization in America, you have only to journey to the Guild Theatre these nights and days and sit before Eugene O'Neill's new trilogy, "Mourning Becomes Electra."

It is a play which towers above the scrubby output of our present-day theatre as the Empire State Building soars above the skyline of Manhattan. Most of its fourteen acts, and particularly its earlier and middle sections, are possessed of a strength and majesty which are equal to its scale. It boasts, too, the kind of radiant austerity which was part of the glory that was Greece.

It is one of the most distinguished, if not the most distinguished, achievements of Mr. O'Neill's career. It is—as the dull word has it—uneven, but so—as the no less dull reverent phrases it—are the Himalayas. ——h are obvious,

---

Eugene O'Neill Explains His Play "The Great God Brown"

Discusses the Mystical Pattern Which Manifests Itself Dimly Behind and Beyond the Words and Actions of the Characters

By Eugene O'Neill

I realize that when a play———ight akes to explaining he thereby s cally places himself "in the at where an open-faced av a play itself of the abstrac derlying it is made impos very nature of that hidde n perhaps it is justifiable hor to confess the myst n which manifests itself a e in "The Great God Brov ind and beyond the word s of the characters.

had hoped the names cho le would give a stror (An old scheme, kespeare and multitu n Anthony"—Dionysus —the creative pagan ife fighting eternal w chistic, life-denying stinnity, as represen ony—the whole strug is modern day in m -creative joy in life rated, rendered abor orality from Pan in phistophels mocki to feel alive; Chr in martyrs for it leading weakly for rthing, even Godh ay it is Cybele, v r, who makes the ity: "Our Fathe ing "Brown" as o inspire "Dion ainty in life f aret" is my im rect descendar " of Faust— with a virtu , properly ob ut the mean ning the rac l" is an inca th Mother d parish in a at patronize o are thus t of their lav a" is the v! materials i g his life empty a a creatur social g ide into "Ah, Wilderness!" he put into

tegral part of his character as the artist. The world is not only blind to ——— beneath but it also sneers ———ask it self re-hristian the na-he same y trans- reality Mephisto-wn's feet, n to de-lmak. but, dies, it is n's feet in as a little ell him a

the creative is he himself n's mask of r is gaining ely whilc in g that crea-tructive by his devil of ort work of ng him apart. ng him until a mask of his vn, before the mask towards s Billy Brown iny one. And on's anguish-Dion had the in the end out l is born, a tor-ich as the dying lief, and at the lips of Cybele. danation regard-It was far from Brown" that this conflicting tides should ever over-ow out of propor-a of the recogni-Dion, Brown, Mar-neant it always to and behind them, gnificance beyond itself through them mysterious words, hey do not them-Anc veat is as an audience to com-lystery—the mystery-man can feel but not meaning of any event any life on earth.

'Ah, Wilderness!' Is Composite of O'Neill's Boyhood

Father's Idiosyncracies, New England Family Life Seen in Play

EUGENE O'NEILL calls his play, "Ah, Wilderness!" which he is playing a return engagement at the Erlanger, "a comedy of recollection." There is a theory, of course, that all of any playwright's plays are written out of recollection, that no one can write without becoming to a certain extent autobiographical. But with "Ah, Wilderness!" this is more than slightly true and Mr. O'Neill admits it.

The Eugene O'Neill legends that have gained headway since he won his way to the position of America's No. 1 playwright concern the adventurous side of his life chiefly. You hear a great deal of the days he spent at sea, "on the beach" in South America, in pot-houses and such. But there is another side. There were the days he spent as a boy in New London, Conn. These are the days that form the background of "Ah, Wilderness."

Eugene O'Neill was just the son of a famous actor then. His father, James O'Neill, had reached the heights on the stage. The boy had, at the time, no ambition that related to the stage. It wasn't until years later, when he was a patient in a sanitarium with nothing to do but think, that his keen mind turned to playwriting.

However, in those New London days he was storing things away in his subconscious mind for a play that was to come later. All his father's little idiosyncracies were being filed in that pigeon-hole. The old gentleman's belief that blue-fish poisoned him and his mother's way of serving it under a "nom de plume" to fool him. The night a friend of the family came for dinner, a little tipsy, and tried to eat the lobster claws and all. All of these things he put into "Ah, Wilderness!"

Breaking away from accepted stage tradition, O'Neill made dramatic history

In the summertime on the Cape, vacationing Broadwayites and critics, too, sought the Provincetowners. To meet the demand, O'Neill wrote one-act plays such as *In the Zone,* which dealt with a ship in submarine waters, and, as vaudeville, brought him steady royalties during World War I. Sturdier fare was *The Long Voyage Home,* a tender tale of a shanghaied sailor. Eugene began to devote his time to full-length plays of great complexity; dissatisfied, he destroyed four separate manuscripts. With the war's end in 1918, he had only *The Straw,* a full-length play drawn from his stay at Gaylord Sanitarium, to show for his labors. Income from *In the Zone* stopped. O'Neill faced new responsibilities, as well as the possibility that he had been a mere flash in the pan.

Agnes Boulton was the daughter of a Philadelphia portrait painter, Edward William Boulton. Coy and diffident about her beauty, she poured herself into short stories and light novels, which found a steady market. Drifting in Greenwich Village, she attempted to deepen her experience; wasn't the Hell Hole a good place for that? She arrived there one night on a lark, and saw at the bar a dark, brooding, handsome man. They were introduced by a mutual friend; O'Neill gave her his entire evening, topping it by saying, "I want to spend every night of my life from now on with you. I mean this. Every night of my life." He married her.

Married and at Provincetown, O'Neill settled into a work schedule. After months of effort, he wrote drama critic Barrett H. Clark the following letter:

May I . . . send you a copy of my long play, *Beyond the Horizon,* in the hope that you will give it a reading? This play is . . . a first serious attempt to do something bigger than my short plays express, and, because of my faith in its sincerity, I would like to submit it to you. I trust it would help to justify your kind encouragement of my work—an encouragement, I assure you, that means the devil of a lot to me.

Clark read the new play with joy and amazement; it was experimental, symbolic and expressionistic, and sincere. Each character in the play was obsessed by a desire for something he could never have—for what lay beyond the horizon.

In *The Straw* this poignance was finely edged in a man declaring his love for a doomed tubercular girl, merely to bring her a last happiness. In the moment of their embrace he realizes he loves her—and must lose her. It seemed to Barrett Clark that *Beyond the Horizon* made the mercurial quality of true happiness more universal. Yes, the play might go over, were it not so long, he wrote Gene.

John Williams agreed to produce the play, but for want of a theater and the proper leading man, months passed without action being taken. A sea play, *Chris Christopherson,* went into production, but was withdrawn by O'Neill in a quarrel over changes. Tense, worried over money, he and Agnes awaited the birth of a child.

With the arrival of Shane Rudraighe O'Neill, the weather seemed to break. "The Event transpired yesterday, and most successfully," Eugene told a friend. "A ten and a half pound boy. . . . His voice already carries further than the Old Man's."

They named him after Shane the Proud, an Irish king. Born in October of 1919, he later kept his mother from the opening February 3, on Broadway at the Morosco Theatre, of the play O'Neill knew would make him or break him.

He had come uptown to the Morosco, and now as the largest audience he had ever drawn streamed in, liberally sprinkled with critics, young Eugene O'Neill virtually hid behind a pillar.

He had written Agnes, "Toward the end, I was so tired and deathly sick of hearing and seeing *Beyond* that I wished it were in hell! It all seemed false and rotten and I wondered why the devil I'd ever written it."

For a week he had suffered insomnia, sleeping four hours a night. The final rehearsal had run twelve hours straight without a break for dinner. He trembled at his observation post as the theater filled.

In came Alexander Woollcott and Heywood Broun, the two most influential critics; in came his father and mother, the sight of whom upset him more. James walked carefully, using a cane; he was seventy-four. Ella, who had gone into seclusion at a convent, had at last broken the morphine habit. They had come to see their son's first real bid for recognition. He would let them down; he knew he would let them down.

The curtains parted.

Andrew, the stalwart, farming brother spoke: "Hey there! Gosh, you do take the prize for day-dreaming! And I see you've toted one of the old books along with you. What is it this time—poetry, I'll bet."

With O'Neill, the audience saw Robert Mayo, the poetic brother, sitting on a fence gazing over the hills toward the sunset. He was a tall, slender young man with a touch of the poet about him, features delicate and refined. He was Eugene O'Neill.

As the long play progressed, the audience remained silent and almost motionless during the action. Robert Mayo declared his dream of going to sea, became chained to a farm instead, fathered a child who died, and then tubercular and broken, rushed out across his ruined land to watch his last dawn. As he died he said, "Look! Isn't it beautiful beyond the hills? I can hear the old voices calling me to come—And this time I'm going! It isn't the end. It's a free beginning—the start of my voyage . . ."

Andrew, the brother, watched. Robert's pathetic, hopeless wife watched. Robert died.

Andrew said, "I—you—we've both made a mess of things! We must try to help each other—and—in time—we'll come to know what's right—And perhaps we—"

Robert's wife, whom Andrew had once loved, remained silent, gazing at him dully. The words had passed her by. "And perhaps *we*—"

The audience rose silently; it was over.

James O'Neill came to Eugene, his face still wet with tears.

"It's all right," he said, "if that's what you want to do, but people come to the theater to forget their troubles, not to be reminded of them." Yet he arranged to meet with his son so they could read the reviews together.

Eugene wrote Agnes, "I suffered tortures! . . . I went out convinced that *Beyond* was a flivver artistically and every other way. That's why I didn't write you last night—I was too depressed. I dreaded to see this day's papers. When I did—lo and behold, in spite of all the handicaps of a rotten first performance, *Beyond* had won. You never saw such notices! There was not a single dissenting voice."

Alexander Woollcott of the *Times* expressed the greatest enthusiasm: "absorbing, significant, and memorable tragedy." Many reviewers complained about the play's length, but likened it to Ibsen, and to a novel by Thomas Hardy.

With hindsight, it may be seen that the play dealt with the difficulty of human communication, a rare theme then, and that its closing line, "And perhaps *we*—" penetrated the darkness like a gleaming shaft of light.

And perhaps *we* . . .

In this final exalting touch, O'Neill had carried the tragedy.

Most reviewers doubted that the play could succeed financially, but it made a long run, confirming that it did more than depress its audience.

At Columbia University in 1920, a three-man board met in secrecy to select a Pulitzer Prize play. They were Hamlin Garland, Richard Burton, and Walter Pritchard Eaton, and they chose O'Neill's *Beyond the Horizon*. Eaton wrote, "*Beyond the Horizon* was not victor without competition. . . . That the judges, though, could have hesitated long over their decision is difficult to imagine, for Mr. O'Neill's drama possesses so conspicuously one merit over all competitors, the merit of a tense, driving, emotional sincerity, imparting to the spectator . . . the sense that the dramatist has been imaginatively at the mercy of his people; not manipulating them so much as manipulated by them."

When O'Neill heard the news, he became defensive: "Oh, a damned medal!" Word of the $1,000 attached sent him whooping with joy.

He was soon to be distracted from his good fortune: in June of that year, James O'Neill entered Lawrence Memorial Hospital, New London. His death was expected soon, for he had had two strokes; instead, he lingered two months. During this time father and son had many talks.

"He suffered. . . . You can imagine what he went through," Eugene wrote. "It was terrible to have to stand by and watch him suffer and not be able to help in any way. . . . His grand old constitution kept him going and forced him to drain the cup of agony to the last bitter drop."

He kept the telegram announcing Gene's Pulitzer Prize at his bedside and showed it to all visitors. To one he said, "Oh, I can die happy, because I think Gene is going to be all right."

His son lingered among his few New London friends. "I thank whatever gods may be that *Beyond* came into its own just in time for him."

James's last words were, "Eugene—I'm going to a better sort of life—this sort of life—here—all froth—no good—rottenness." To the end, James O'Neill lamented his imprisonment in the role of Edmond Dantès.

The Count of Monte Cristo was dead. His son read the many obituaries as though they were reviews. Writers rediscovered James's great days on stage with Forrest, Edwin Booth, and the others. They told of his great promise, and his steadfast devotion to the stage. They found him with the greats, in his way, a titan in his own right.

Eugene took his warning and promised to be true to the best that was in him. This he did, by his own lights, though it was to mean leaving another wife and turning his back on his children.

In his long career his plays would be translated into every major language; he would win a Nobel Prize and more Pulitzers. He would change the sound of American drama, and exert his influence throughout the world.

Winning an earlier Nobel Prize, novelist Sinclair Lewis told the Swedish academy, "And had you chosen Eugene O'Neill, who has done nothing much in the American drama save to transform it utterly in ten or twelve years from a false world of neat and competent trickery into a world of splendor, fear, and greatness, you would have been reminded that he had done something far worse than scoffing, that he had seen life as something not to be neatly arranged in a study, but as terrifying, magnificent and often quite horrible, a thing akin to a tornado, an earthquake or a devastating fire."

John Mason Brown once said when a play of O'Neill's was called *uneven*, "It is—as the dull word has it—uneven, but so—as the no less dull retort phrases it—are the Himalayas."

O'Neill was a man who went through the world listening to people, listening to *us*.

So the dramatists tell us what we have said, for we are too busy to hear, and what we have been trying to say. The actors put it on, where we can come together to find it. And perhaps *we*—

O'Neill: Afterview

YOU CAN STAND TODAY on the clean Cape Cod sands of Peaked Hill Bar near Provincetown, Massachusetts, where the Coast Guard station that served Eugene O'Neill as house and studio once stood, and with the ebb of sand underfoot, sense the will of things substantial to slide into the sea.

Which the Peaked Hill Bar station eventually did.

In the town, still an eastern headquarters for artistic people, old men tell of a young O'Neill vividly remembered as rebellious, drinking, writing.

"I used to bail him out of jail regularly; him and his friends; but he was usually very quiet, and we liked him. I'll tell you, he was like many of the kids today, who want to change things."

In the museum at the *Mayflower*'s landfall, the memorabilia of O'Neill's historic stay on that peninsula are displayed near an exhibition of evidence that Norsemen first found America here. In the morning it is the sunlight of Europe which bathes this shore, and we see the ships coming out of dim history, tentative, and probably leaking. And we see a snapshot of the little house of Agnes and Eugene sliding to sea, trying to become a boat.

It was to the Norse that Eugene cleaved; to Strindberg and Ibsen, and to the sea. They pulled him toward the depths and into the currents of the soul. He wrote psychologically, but did not understand himself. He was being drawn toward a vortex. There were almost uncountable successes: *Desire Under the Elms, The Great God Brown, Strange Interlude, Mourning Becomes Electra, Ah, Wilderness!, A Touch of the Poet, The Iceman Cometh, Long Day's Journey Into Night, A Moon for the Misbegotten.* Out of the luscious years of the twenties came fame and a great deal of money.

With success, he withdrew, by stages, from life. Agnes and the children became a burden on his writing. Having established them in a magnificent estate on Bermuda, O'Neill fell in love with an actress of storybook beauty, Carlotta Monterey, who had acted in one of his plays. No one could stall his love for Carlotta, though many close show-business friends tried.

His flight continued, this time to France, the land of Monte Cristo. At Saint-Antoine-du-Rocher he rented a forty-five-room chateau called Le Plessis, and in it constructed a sort of writer's "throne," complete with all sorts of writing attachments and aids permitting him the long hours of concentration he desired. At Le Plessis he remained three years, working, walking the countryside, visiting occasionally in the village.

Return to America meant an island retreat off the coast of Georgia, and an isolation almost as complete as though he had been imprisoned like Dumas' character in Chateau d'If.

As years went by O'Neill proceeded toward the vanishing point of his own past. He had once done his best to reconcile himself to his own children, even encouraging his first son, Eugene, Jr., who became a scholar and his friend. Now he withdrew from him too, contributing, in all likelihood, to the young man's suicide.

Nothing interested O'Neill but the ghosts of his childhood. Two years of brooding and concentration yielded *Long Day's Journey Into Night* in which he bared the still rupturing sore of his youthful feelings toward his father and mother. Reliving the past was absolute torture. "At times I thought he'd go mad," his wife remembered. "It was terrifying to watch his suffering."

He ordered the manuscript sealed in red wax, not to be opened for twenty-five years, an order which, fortunately, has been disobeyed.

During the next decade, interest in O'Neill declined. He had become ill with Parkinson's disease, which affected his ability to move. At Marblehead, Massachusetts, one night, he staggered across snowy ground near the ocean. He was found prostrate, a leg broken. Many have theorized that he wished to find peace by plunging into the cold waves. As his illness progressed, he spoke often to his wife of death by euthanasia or suicide.

Once he announced that none must be allowed to finish his plays. He ordered her to bring his unfinished manuscripts, and together they tore them into pieces.

"He could only tear a few pages at a time, because of his tremor," she remembered. "So I helped him. We tore up all the manuscripts together, bit by bit. It took hours. After a pile of torn pages had collected, I'd throw it into the fire. It was awful. It was like tearing up children."

O'Neill's finished works included *The Emperor Jones, All God's Chillun Got Wings, Beyond the Horizon, The Long Voyage Home, Bound East for Cardiff, Anna Christie, The Fountain,* and *Marco Millions.*

He was awarded the Nobel Prize for Literature in 1936.

O'Neill asks for all who have acted and written for the stage, "What shall men and women say, what shall they do, what shall they believe?" When he no

Eugene spent happy hours at the ancient player piano, a gift from his wife, Carlotta

longer believed, he decided he must destroy his work. If he did not, the audience might decide by going out of the theater.

People write plays partly because people will act in them, and people act in them because people will watch. Something tempts us all to assume the character of another, to "playact," or to change our daily manner or role. Those in the theater are most adept at this. But characters and lines are created which live for centuries, affecting generations. The effect is enhanced by films and television, so that entire societies are given models of thought, action, and manner. The theater lives close to the root of society itself.

By what process will the compulsions of the creative minds be refined? Probably by the education of audiences. The worst in O'Neill or Forrest was a showman catering to sensation. The best was a genius holding up a mirror to humanity. In the end, the best audiences will decide the best plays. You the audience may even write and act in them now that the conventions of the theater are being changed so drastically.

In certain experimental improvisations called "happenings," the audience is actor and playwright. Will a day be reached when the conventional theater as we know it is obsolete? Perhaps. But as long as children make-believe, they will grow into men who prefer to assume a role—as Count of Monte Cristo, or Hamlet, or the Emperor Jones instead of being their own drab selves, and other men will empathize and forget their own identity for those few brief hours while they watch entranced. And the Shakespeares and the O'Neills will unite the two in the shared glory of great plays.

Bibliography

GENERAL

Gassner, John, *Theatre at the Crossroads: Plays and Playwrights of the Mid-century American Stage.* Holt, Rinehart, & Winston, Inc., 1960.

Jefferson, Joseph, *Autobiography of Joseph Jefferson.* London, 1889.

Macgowan, Kenneth, *Footlights Across America: Towards a National Theater.* Harcourt Brace, 1929.

Marshall, Herbert, and Stock, Mildred, *Ira Aldridge: The Negro Tragedian.* Southern Illinois University Press, 1968.

Morris, Lloyd L., *Curtain Time: The Story of the American Theater.* Random House, Inc., 1953.

Quinn, Arthur Hobson, *A History of the American Drama: From the Beginning to the Civil War.* Appleton-Century Crofts, Inc., 1943.

Quinn, Arthur Hobson (ed.), *Representative American Plays.* Appleton-Century-Crofts, Inc., 1953.

The Robinson Locke Collection of Dramatic Scrapbooks, Theatre Collection, The Library and Museum of the Performing Arts, The New York Public Library at Lincoln Center, New York.

Taubman, Howard, *The Making of the American Theatre.* Coward-McCann, Inc., 1965.

EDWIN FORREST

Barrett, Lawrence, *Edwin Forrest.* 1881.

Moody, Richard, *Edwin Forrest: First Star of the American Stage.* Alfred A. Knopf, Inc., 1960.

THE BOOTHS

Clarke, Asia Booth, *The Elder and the Younger Booth*. 1882.

Ferguson, William J., *I Saw Booth Shoot Lincoln*. Houghton Mifflin Company, 1930.

Grossman, Edwina Booth, *Edwin Booth: Recollections by His Daughter and letters to her and to his friends*. The Century Company, 1894.

Kimmel, Stanley Preston, *The Mad Booths of Maryland*. The Bobbs-Merrill Company, Inc., 1940.

Miller, Ernest Conrad, *John Wilkes Booth—Oilman*. The Exposition Press, 1947.

Ruggles, Eleanor, *Prince of Players: Edwin Booth*. W. W. Norton & Company, Inc., 1953.

THE O'NEILLS

Boulton, Agnes, *Part of a Long Story*. Doubleday & Company, Inc., 1958.

Bowen, Croswell, and O'Neill, Shane, *The Curse of the Misbegotten*. McGraw-Hill Book Company, Inc., 1959.

Cargill, Oscar; Fagin, N. Bryllian; and Fisher, William J. (eds.), *O'Neill and His Plays: Four Decades of Criticism*. New York University Press, 1959.

Gassner, John (ed.), *O'Neill: A Collection of Critical Essays*. Prentice-Hall, Inc., 1964.

Gelb, Arthur and Barbara, *O'Neill*. Harper & Brothers, 1962.

Sheaffer, Louis, *O'Neill, Son and Playwright*. Little, Brown and Company, 1968.

Index